Praise for *Future Shaper*

'In today's world of mixed signals and rapid change, we need our leaders to evolve their skills and step up to a new decade, where use of technology and talent will be at the heart of competitive advantage. Niamh O'Keeffe's future shaper framework and approach provide a structured guide and advice on how to navigate leadership complexity and stay relevant. This book is a valuable and practical resource. It is a highly recommended read that will deliver a worthwhile ongoing leadership dividend.' MARK SPELMAN, HEAD OF THOUGHT LEADERSHIP, WORLD ECONOMIC FORUM

'*Future Shaper* insightfully describes the challenges of leadership in a rapidly accelerating technology-centric world of change, and is replete with practical frameworks for reflecting on what it takes to shape an organization's future in the face of systemic uncertainty and changing workforce expectations. It is a thought-provoking and practical guide to the serious student of leadership.' TIM BREENE, CEO WORLD RELIEF, AND CO-AUTHOR OF *JUMPING THE S-CURVE*

'Compelling insights for the modern business leader on what it takes to be successful in our uncertain times.' JOHN BOLZE, SENIOR MANAGING DIRECTOR, ACCENTURE

Future Shaper

*How leaders can take charge
in an uncertain world*

Niamh O'Keeffe

Kogan Page
INSPIRE

First published in Great Britain and the United States in 2020 by Kogan Page Limited

2nd Floor, 45 Gee Street	122 W 27th St, 10th Floor	4737/23 Ansari Road
London	New York, NY 10001	Daryaganj
EC1V 3RS	USA	New Delhi 110002
United Kingdom		India

www.koganpage.com

Kogan Page books are printed on paper from sustainable forests.

ISBNs

Hardback	978 1 78966 220 7
Paperback	978 1 78966 218 4
Ebook	978 1 78966 219 1

British Library Cataloguing-in-Publication Data

A CIP record for this book is available from the British Library.

Library of Congress Cataloging-in-Publication Data

LCCN: 2019057282

Typeset by Integra Software Services, Pondicherry
Print production managed by Jellyfish
Printed and bound by CPI Group (UK) Ltd, Croydon, CR0 4YY

Contents

About the author

Niamh O'Keeffe is a leadership advisor, author and the founder of First100 and The Prosper Leadership Academy (www.prosperleadershipacademy.com). Niamh has a track record of over 25 years' career experience in leadership advisory services – including strategy consulting, executive search and leadership coaching. Niamh's insights in this book are based on her experience as a trusted advisor to chief executives and working with senior leaders on key moments in their leadership role lifecycle: how to get promoted, how to have a great first 100 days, how to stay the course and legacy projects. Niamh's client list spans multiple industries and includes advising leaders of entrepreneurial ventures in London and New York, as well as senior executives at global corporations like Accenture, Microsoft and Oliver Wyman Group.

Niamh is driven by a purposeful mission to improve the quality of leadership in the world.

> I hope to inspire you with a fresh take on your leadership role in the face of an increasingly uncertain and complex world. This is about evolving your leadership intelligence to empower you; to help you rise above the overwhelm; and to shape a better future for yourself and for everyone.

The second edition of Niamh's best-selling book *Your First 100 Days: How to make maximum impact in your new leadership role* was published in 2019. Niamh's other published books include *Lead your Team in your First 100 Days* (2013), *Your Next Role: How to get ahead and get promoted* (2016) and *Stepping Up: How to accelerate your leadership potential* (2017).

Acknowledgements

Many thanks to editor Chris Cudmore for his encouragement, patience and good counsel.

Thank you to Omar Abbosh for inspiring this book. Thank you to my clients for trusting me to advise them during their leadership journey. With appreciation to Eimee Kuah for being my long-term advisor and ongoing source of support. As always, a special mention to my daughter, Meera, whose bright smile and beautiful spirit inspire me every day.

Make or break your leadership career
Why you should read this book

In a world of distractions and overwhelm, why would you choose to spend a few hours of your precious time reading this book? The most compelling reasons I can give you are that this book will improve your leadership intelligence, help you succeed in your leadership career and empower you to shape a better future for everyone. If you are ambitious and feel that you have unfulfilled leadership potential, then read on.

In past times, leaders were the ones who had maximum access to information and were better able to predict what would happen next. Employees had a reassuring (even if false) sense of security that top executives knew how to solve all the difficult challenges and problems. There was sufficient stability to develop 10-year plans, and more clarity on exactly how to steer the business. Until recently, leadership has been about setting out a definitive strategy and instructing people on how to execute it. No one would buy that approach any more. I don't have to tell you that we are living in interesting times! The world has changed, unpredictability is the new predictability, and traditional rules for how to lead do not apply any more. The type of leadership intelligence required is no longer limited to strategic capability, emotional intelligence and good communication skills – instead it is about a further evolution to whole new set of leadership intelligence fundamentals and an upskilling in the new leadership traits required for the types of challenges and uncertainty we face now.

This book is my attempt at the new leadership intelligence playbook needed to deal with all the threats and opportunities ahead. Leadership theory needs to catch up and, for me, the central point is empowerment. How can you be empowered to take charge in an uncertain world? Although it sounds counter-intuitive, I believe you have more control and more choice than you realize. This empowered mindset is what sets apart the leader from the follower, and indeed what sets apart the leader from the machine. This book is about gaining better leadership intelligence in an increasingly artificial intelligence world. I use the term 'future shaping' to describe the type of leadership needed now. The future shaper leader is prepared to face up to the challenges of today and decide what to do about them in order to create a better tomorrow. This book offers a blueprint to help guide leaders on how to take back control, proactively future shape and achieve great success.

Behind complex narratives on the future outlook of the global economy lies a more honest diagnosis of the current state of play – which is that we are experiencing a crisis of leadership. And like any crisis, only the most adaptable will survive. In this book I decode what it will take to survive and thrive as a great leader now, and I offer you inspiration and insight on how to skill up for the journey ahead.

In brief summary, the future shaping leadership intelligence playbook builds your capacity to:

- Step back to get perspective and see the bigger picture.
- Realize you have the power to shape the future.
- Stop feeling afraid of unknowns and 'wildcard' events.
- Empower yourself to lead; don't wait for permission or the right job title.
- Apply a new leadership intelligence framework and cultivate more relevant traits.

The future shaping leadership intelligence framework will steer you on how to shape the future you desire:

- Establish your preferred future outcome.
- Convince people to follow you.
- Be resilient and stay the course.

- Nurture successful teams and deliver great results.
- Power up your network and multiply your impact.

To support your application of the future shaper framework, I invite you to cultivate a new set of essential leadership traits. I help you to become more:

- fearless, unconventional, tenacious, unifying, resilient, empathetic;
- super-adaptable, hard-working, authentic, proactive, energizing, resourceful.

The total opportunity for you will be to create a positive leadership ripple effect for you and the world around you:

- Empower yourself and others.
- Join forces with like-minded leaders, and change the world.
- Succeed in your leadership career and make an impact.

I have peppered the book with quotes and examples of iconic future shapers (past and present) to help inspire you along the way and to ground my ideas in real people, real experience and real results.

Surprisingly, leaders don't think enough about the task of leading, or the methodology or approach that we take to the task of leading. Leaders face very challenging situations and typically get busy leading in a very organic self-directed way. When the pressure mounts up, this can involve doing the managing, or even doing the doing and not really leading at all. Ask yourself, ask your peers, ask your boss – what is your approach to leadership? You will get a patchwork of answers that range from someone's guiding philosophy, eg 'Who dares, wins' to a set of core values, eg 'I believe in authenticity, and respect for the individual', to some key mantras that can be a bit reductive, eg 'It's all about people' or 'It's all about EQ, not IQ'. Rarely ever, will someone respond by explaining the framework or actual set of steps they take to approaching their leadership task. Why not? Because they don't have one. For some inexplicable reason we are missing the 'manual' for leadership. Yes, there are thousands of books on leadership, and hundreds of examples of great leaders, but somehow it never quite got captured into a useful methodology that stuck. Perhaps leaders rail against the very idea of process skills for leadership and being 'constrained' by a methodology – because they prefer to see leadership as an art and not a science. But without a clearly defined approach to leadership, it is all too easy to get derailed and lose sight of what you are supposed to be focused on.

A new intelligent framework and playbook on how to lead will help steady us. This missing manual or intelligent playbook is what I want to offer you. The framework starts by asking you for total clarity on your future preferable outcome, and an explanation of the further four key fundamental levers that help you to power up and convert this preferable outcome into a more predictable outcome. And, finally, I describe the critical wraparound of leadership traits you need to cultivate to become a true future shaper and properly apply the levers.

Once you have mastered the future shaping approach on how to lead, you will feel more empowered. You will be clear on what you need to do. You will be focused on your big-picture vision, your key strategic outcomes and will deal with everything in the context of the higher goals you set out to achieve. You are less likely to get derailed from your key priorities – or if/when you do, you will have a methodology for lifting yourself back up out of the detail, in order to refocus on the bigger picture and the key strategic outcomes you are trying to shape. Rather than feeling relentlessly buffeted and at the mercy of events, trying to predict the unpredictable or waiting passively to see what will happen next – you have an approach to follow, which helps you to take back control, empower yourself and decide what kind of future you want to create. Rather than wasting time dealing with lists of never-ending problems and issues, you can rise above the overwhelm and set the agenda. You will feel better when you empower yourself to step up as a future shaper, take charge and make decisions – and when you have this better sense of control over what is happening, this will further empower and embolden you. Stop waiting and start creating! This is an empowering rally cry to step up and take more leadership action to shape a better future for you, your organization and ultimately the world.

The real value of this book is that it is a catalyst for sustainable leadership success. It has four distinct strengths; its holistic approach, to people and context; its pragmatism, in blending useful ideas and top tips with the reality of our uncertain business environment; and its framework, to provide a foundation and structure in which individuals are enabled, and can build, to achieve their personal leadership potential. Finally, like all good ideas and approaches, it is empowering and actionable and allows individuals like you, dear reader, to immediately deliver benefits for yourself and others.

Thank you for investing the time to read this book, and I wish you well as you start your journey towards becoming a future shaper leader and fulfilling your leadership potential.

PART ONE

Leadership overwhelm

CHAPTER ONE

The exhilaration and exhaustion of being a leader today

To put it simply, leadership has become more complicated

As a leader, you have to navigate a way forward in the face of an exciting technology and AI revolution, and against a backdrop of geopolitical turmoil and societal change. New challenges and new possibilities emerge every day. The opportunities seem so limitless – if only we had the time to think about them! The relentless pace of change keeps us stimulated, and also ensures we can never stay complacent – not at the weekend, not at quarter end, not at year end and maybe never again.

This is an unsettling and unstable time for the world economically, politically and socially. Let's name-check all the complex macro forces at play as a backdrop to business leadership today: global economy, climate change, corruption, terrorism, mass migration, populism. At times, it can be overwhelming listening to the morning news and your day has only just begun. It sometimes feels as if the world is spinning out of control and this inevitably impacts our role as business leaders. Current watchwords in business today are 'uncertainty' and 'disruption'. Business media and industry commentators are trying to look around corners and producing ever more anxiety-inducing reports like 'how to manage the trust deficit' and 'how to lead in the age of artificial intelligence'.

No one wants to admit it, but leaders at the top are frightened – there are fewer knowns and the pace of change ushered in by the Fourth Industrial Revolution is so fast-moving that it is hard to keep up. Leaders realize their businesses are facing potential sudden collapse because of inadequate speed of response to digital and AI threats and opportunities, resulting in our current innovative disruption environment. Worse than sudden collapse are the more common occurrences we all witness, such as relentless undermining and eroding of profit year on year, when the tide turns in an industry and players stuck in traditional business models just cannot seem to respond, for example our high-street shops in the face of consumers' switch to online shopping.

Leaders today have so much to deal with. Even if you love your leadership role, a sense of leadership vertigo may creep in from time to time, when the stakes get higher and the pressure mounts up. Perhaps the word 'overwhelmed' sums up how you are feeling some or most of the time?

You will have your own experience and perspective on the unique pressures in your role. Here is a top ten list of what I have noticed, in terms of the complex challenges that constantly permeate the leadership time and efforts of business leaders today:

- Navigating through global uncertainty and unpredictability, and not knowing what macro or micro shocks and disruptions are around the next corner.
- Anticipating the opportunity and impact of artificial intelligence on how to go to market, and how to lead people and teams.
- Managing the complexity of an ever-expanding, shifting ecosystem of partners, suppliers and customers in our increasingly interconnected world.

- Dealing with an increased speed and volume of data, information and communication, and how to filter through it to focus on the key relevant facts.
- Having to be in touch all the time, whether that's via social media or across different time zones, and being expected to respond and make leadership decisions immediately.
- Figuring out how to create a more inclusive environment in order to benefit from a range of more diverse experiences and fresh points of view.
- Satisfying the expectations of the millennial workforce at a time when employee expectations have become ever more demanding. The younger generation are asserting their desire for more meaningful work and want to feel simultaneously fulfilled, stimulated and stretched as well as enjoying an appropriate work–life balance.
- When budgets are restricted, the effort of being asked to achieve more with fewer resources, while still motivating and inspiring a workforce to deliver to deadlines and not burn out along the way.
- Addressing customer and societal demands that business becomes more transparent and becomes a greater force for good.
- The challenge of setting priorities in face of such relentless change.

To put it simply, leadership has become increasingly complicated. Let's examine some of the broader themes in more detail.

An unpredictable future amplified by the Fourth Industrial Revolution

If there is a pattern, it seems to be that unpredictability is the new predictability. We start off expecting one outcome, and we inevitably get another – whether that is the collapse of institutions too big to fail or the unexpected outcomes of political elections. How can leaders be expected to plan for their businesses knowing to expect a series of unpredictable international and domestic economic unknowns? When I first started out on my career, the world of work seemed to be a more stable place and certainly strategic work plans were more linear. We set out a ten-year plan; we broke it into timeline goals across horizons of what needed to be achieved within five years, within three years, within one year. That doesn't seem like a realistic way to plan any more. Now it is fair to say we have shifted from linear to a more organic and opportunistic spaghetti-shaped planning landscape!

There are still attempts to imagine what the world will look like in the future. From a possible extinction event, or apocalyptic visions of a doomed future and nuclear wars, food and water shortages, and widespread social discontent, to the utopian vision of leisure and abundance for all on Earth and on Mars with humans coexisting collaboratively with their benign robot counterparts... and all things in between. But, of course, we just don't know. And because we don't know what the future will bring, we seem to struggle to confidently set out any stakes in the ground.

What we do know is that the Fourth Industrial Revolution is under way. The First Industrial Revolution introduced the use of steam power to mechanize production. The Second Industrial Revolution saw a number of ground-breaking inventions in transport, telecommunications and manufacturing, including the use of electric power to generate mass production. The Third Industrial Revolution brought the internet and other technological innovations, which have ushered humanity into the digital era. Today, society is undergoing a Fourth Industrial Revolution, an age in which scientific and technological breakthroughs are disrupting industries, blurring geographical boundaries, challenging existing regulatory frameworks, and even redefining what it means to be human. Emerging technologies such as artificial intelligence (AI), blockchain, drones and precision medicine are swiftly changing lives and transforming businesses and societies, inevitably posing new risks and raising ethical concerns. The Fourth Industrial Revolution, says Klaus Schwab, in his book of the same name (Schwab, 2016), will impact all disciplines, economies and industries at an unprecedented rate and is characterized by new technologies fusing the physical, digital and biological worlds. The Fourth Industrial Revolution brings tremendous opportunities. However, it also raises the question of who will succeed and who will fail in the 2020s and the decades ahead. Only the fittest organizations and most adaptable leaders will survive.

Leaders under constant threat alert: 'disrupt or be disrupted'

You are under constant pressure because your business model is under constant pressure. On the one hand, the advances in technology and the AI revolution are making our lives easier. On the other hand, limitless consumer and business possibilities open up and there is so much more pressure to compete at an organizational level. 'Disrupt or be disrupted' is a clanging chime of hope and doom ringing in our ears, which means that leaders are under constant threat alert and constant pressure to think ahead, to look around corners, to be creative, to innovate and to make changes. For example, the new digital payment systems threaten traditional banking. It is interesting to note that a robust global company like Diageo has a strategy of investing in entrepreneurial disruptors, within their own industry, so they can stay close to the entrepreneurial frontier and stay ahead of what might be coming around the corner at them.

You are under constant pressure because your business model is under constant pressure.

The message on disruption and innovation is loud and clear. Leaders are now hyper-aware of the threat potential and the need to convert any crisis into new opportunities, fast. Apart from being hyper-aware, hyper-alert to the point of paranoia, what else should we do to take charge and act? While we rush around on adrenalin, are we missing the bigger picture and neglecting to pay attention to cultivating the appropriate leadership skills needed for this kind of relentless dynamic business environment?

Even if your company is the disruptor, you can't be complacent. We see the tech companies under more scrutiny than ever before. They are having to grow up in front of our eyes and navigate issues like maintaining users' trust. If you belong to a more traditional company, a key leadership challenge is how to rethink, reimagine and reinvent your business model, harness big data and new technologies, and make a wise pivot towards the new and the future. Just inserting or layering on artificial intelligence to existing processes and systems won't cut it – or, at a minimum is a lost opportunity for the full potential of what could be achieved. Of course, it's still all about the customer, and it always will be. But the competition to reach that customer and fulfil their needs will be played out with new gusto in terms of how fast you can harness new technologies to identify and serve customer needs, integrate learning loops into processes and act on insights in real time. There are new enablers in town, and more coming. This is so exciting! But also so many 'what ifs' and inherent threats if we don't master this, or are not the first off the blocks, or fail to step up as leaders to take advantage of the new possibilities.

Seismic shifts such as anticipating how to lead in the age of artificial intelligence

Many top executives have started to feel a bit adrift in today's climate of disruption and new digital and AI revolution. Many are already struggling to lead through disruption and – next – fast coming down the track is the question of how to anticipate the threats and opportunities that AI is bringing. Leading through disruption is being quickly superseded by fresh challenges on how to lead in the age of artificial intelligence.

Should you be worried about the impact artificial intelligence will have on how you go to market in the future and how you organize and lead your workforce? Of course! But how can you plan for something you don't yet understand? Even the renowned theoretical physicist, Stephen Hawking, said that AI could be either the best or worst invention humanity has ever made. Hawking said developments in AI have been so great that the machines will one day be more dominant than human beings. So, plenty of room for ongoing future uncertainty there!

Every era of technological change has been met with resistance, but ultimately it has also brought about a huge amount of progress and freedom for workforces and employers. Leaders will have to rise above any fear and resistance to search for the opportunities brought by AI. Successful leadership will involve educating the workforce about how automation and overhauling the existing operational model can result in more enjoyable, strategic and creative job roles, and how people and machines working together will bring more productivity and increased revenues. Leaders will have to figure out how AI becomes a competitive advantage. They will have to find ways to soothe fears from workers about inevitable job losses – and reskill people for the new types of roles that will emerge, such as augmented reality architect, avatar relationship manager, digital identity planner, 3D organ designer and many more. Leaders will need the self-confidence to step into the unknown and make decisions with next to no certainty. It will be a curious set-up when we get to the point of having to learn how to manage and lead robots, as well as managing and leading people. We will need to get used to having new types of colleagues who aren't human, and also learn how to get the best out of them.

With all this in mind, it is understandable that leaders are unnerved and finding it increasingly difficult to keep up with the challenges of leading in today's complicated fast-moving environment.

Emergence of ecosystems that require a new type of borderless leadership

Leadership has become more borderless. Previously we were just concerned with our team, our operating unit, our organization and our market. We enjoyed a fairly narrow and bounded definition of what we had to take care of. That too has changed, and we are now transcending traditional borders as we witness the emergence of powerful ecosystems – clusters of companies that form new collaborative relationships, who choose to build on synergies and mutual wins rather than the traditional 'I win, you lose' style of competing. Intersections where we can all win are now much more in vogue – but how to establish these ecosystems, how to be a leader within one, how to co-evolve, how to manage the dynamics and the uncontrollables within these new arrangements require an evolved set of leadership skills.

As you already know, your ecosystem entities are the organizations that your company depends on in order to do its business. However, the ecosystem approach goes beyond the traditional supply chains to examine the more complex web in which a company operates. Business ecosystems are complex and ever changing. New companies enter, exit and take on different roles constantly. So it's impossible to fully map an ecosystem. Leaders have realized that they need to find a way to understand and develop insights into their ecosystems to help them make smarter strategic decisions.

Leadership in an ecosystem is about convening, connecting, encouraging and enabling. Within an ecosystem it is about collective success. This is a very different mentality required for leaders who may have grown up in a very aggressive and combative culture of competition. Traditional thinking envisions companies as rivals, battling each other for dominance and profit. Today's organizations operate in a more complex world. They integrate competition and cooperation in innovative and unexpected ways and they need each other in order to survive.

The switch in leadership skill set required is profound – and requires an unlearning and a relearning of leadership approach, which could confound the most experienced and seasoned executives. As well as leading your teams, it is also about how to influence your networks. Is it time to rewrite all the management and leadership text books? How can leaders be expected to simply reorient, reskill, reframe and transform their approach to competition – and yet, here we are and this is the ask. Reinventing the market system surely requires a reinvention of our leadership models and behaviours.

Vast amounts of information but fewer knowns and faster decisions

We are suffering from data and information overload. Ironically, the more information we have, the harder it is to make a decision. The more information we have to wade through, the less time is available to figure out the insight. We need to make decisions faster, but when a situation is complex, decisions become paralysed in analysis as we are tempted to wait for more information to support or refute a course of action. There are technologies to help filter the data, but in the end the insights come from a leader who understands the context and has good judgement on how to understand and apply the data to their marketplace. When the information tap just keeps flowing, we sometimes adopt a grab-and-go mentality – grabbing what's available, making suboptimal decisions as we go and having the 'security' of blaming the data afterwards.

Leaders are faced with how to make the complex simple and actionable – and how to involve the right people in the decision making so that they don't alienate key stakeholders on the journey. Making decisions in today's climate seems to involve a robust strength of character, an agile mind and good judgement to know when to wait and when to act. Fortunately like every other skill, good leaders become more skilled with practice – but the pace is relentless and that in itself takes a toll.

Leaders are faced with how to make the complex simple and actionable.

There is always a trade-off between finding the right answer and making a decision. Simple contexts, properly assessed, have clear cause and effect options and getting to the right answer requires only straightforward decision making. Complicated contexts, which is where contemporary business sits today, may contain multiple 'right' answers, and there may not be a clear relationship between cause and effect. This is the realm of 'known unknowns' and 'unknown unknowns'. In other words, we don't know what the effect of our decision may be – so there may be no right answer. There is no perfect set of data to drive these kinds of complex decisions. In the end, the onus is on the leader to feel the fear and make the decision anyway– make your decision, wait, sense and then respond.

Couple this up with the new social media demands of being available to give and receive live Twitter and other social media commentary 24-7 and it is no wonder that our minds are not clear and we don't always make great decisions in the moment. Everything is live and immediate – people want the answer and they want it now. It can be very challenging for leaders to step back and pause, and reflect on the best way forward. It requires a very agile mind to incorporate the new data points that arise today, which mean we either do or don't change our strategy by close of play. I exaggerate of course, but, as you know, not by much.

Post-digital leadership: understanding what's next in technology and its impact on role

There is no need to say you lead a 'digital business'. If you're still in business, investing in digital is understood. Digital itself is no longer differentiating. With every business investing heavily in digital technologies, how will leaders compete in the future? Leaders in business today don't just need to know what represents cutting-edge technology, they need to be quick adaptors, and quick embracers of all that is new and all that is possible. Thanks to the power of digital now and post-digital next, the next era will be one of massive customer, employee and societal expectations. It will be an era of equally tremendous possibility: to deliver for any moment in any reality.

Let's have fun with the acronyms now. Have you mastered your understanding of SMAC as a core competency (social, mobile, analytics and cloud) and a foundation to rotate to what's next? Because, as you know, when it comes to enterprise-level technology strategies, companies can never stop moving. At this point, the failure to complete a mastery of SMAC will leave businesses unable to serve even the most basic demands of a post-digital world. But success will unlock boundless future opportunity. Distributed ledger technology, Artificial intelligence, extended Reality and Quantum computing (DARQ) are already having an impact in disparate areas of enterprise. DARQ technologies will drive the post-digital wave, but catching that wave will only be possible with the firm foundation of SMAC. Looking even further down the road? DARQ technologies will enable innovation in core aspects of the business and will be foundational for whatever comes after that. These are the next set of new technologies to spark a step change, letting businesses and leaders reimagine entire industries.

It is thrilling to be on this rollercoaster of exponential possibilities but only if leaders can have one foot in the future and one in the present day as we navigate our leadership strategies across with the new, the now and the next. Future-minded leaders know that they will need not only every digital tool in their current arsenal to succeed, they'll also need new ones.

As leaders, we are also trying to figure out the full potential of the 'human + machine' workforce. How do we bring together people, culture, leadership, organization and technology? Can we align a complex set of dynamics under a common purpose and lead them to maximum organizational and personal potential? All great questions, but I'm not sure how easy it is to provide the answers, or to implement them.

The challenges of satisfying and managing expectations of a millennial workforce

Also known as Generation Y or the Net Generation, millennials are the demographic cohort that directly follows Generation X. The term 'millennials' is usually considered to apply to individuals who reached adulthood around the turn of the 21st century – although precise delineation varies from one source to another, eg birth dates between 1976 and 2004. As a contemporary leader in the 2020s, you are either a millennial or are running a team made up mostly of millennials. This generation has a set of expectations and demands that can put their leader under pressure. For example, workplace satisfaction matters more to millennials than monetary compensation, and flexibility or 'work–life balance' is often considered essential. This is very admirable and reasonable at one level – until the pressures of deadlines kick in, and then what?

Millennials are less likely than previous generations to put up with an unpleasant work environment and much more likely to use social networking to broadcast their concerns. On the other hand, satisfied millennials are often employee advocates for the organizations they work for, providing honest, free – and convincing – public relations. Millennials are also more concerned about social justice and will not support institutions that they see as being in conflict with social and economic equality. They are very focused on the social responsibility profile of any organization they're considering working for. They want to know your company's stance on the environment, on community involvement and social responsibility. All of this plays a large role in whether or not they're interested in staying employed at your company, or coming to work for your brand.

Millennials, in many cases, have grown up under a style of parenting that supported individual empowerment, where the kids were almost always included in family decision making. This carries through at work and millennials are seeking affirmation that they're more than a cog in a massive corporate machine. The leader of millennials will be under constant pressure to try to create opportunities that give millennials the chance to take responsibility and find success on a micro level before they move on to larger roles. Millennials also may expect a timetable for career advancement that comes off as unrealistic to their bosses: as one company leader said off the record, 'Great people are coming into our industry who are highly educated and who all want to be directors of everything immediately' (Solomon, 2016).

The millennials assert their desires for more meaningful work and want to feel simultaneously fulfilled, stimulated, stretched, as well as enjoying an appropriate work–life balance. Top talent expect hyper-personalized employee experiences – and expect to define their own day-to-day details, as well as career paths within an organization. Millennials prefer flatter structures, want maximum participation in decision making early on, expect opportunities to make an impact from the outset – and yet are criticized for having a lack of resilience (the so-called 'snowflake' generation) in the face of obstacles, challenges and hardship.

A new generation brings a fresh energy and fresh opportunity for progress. However, this also brings a complete reframe of the leadership dynamic from the traditional model of a 'subordinate' employee, and can add extra pressure to an already pressurized leadership role.

An accelerating sustainability agenda and concern for the global environment

If not already fully tuned in, business leaders need to take swift notice of accelerating consumer and employee passions for sustainability and concern for the health of the planet. At a minimum, top leadership need to develop a sustainability strategy and take steps to do no harm. However, top leadership should also realize that the ability to deliver products and services sustainably and meet the needs of today's global population without sacrificing the needs of future generations represents one of the biggest business opportunities since the Industrial Revolution. The Business & Sustainable Development Commission (2017) suggests that the economic opportunities presented by achieving the UN Sustainable Development Goals (UN SDGs) is valued at more than $12 trillion. As companies around the world operate in a rapidly changing global ecosystem and are held to increasingly demanding environmental and social standards, the executives that lead these companies need to understand how these environmental and social factors affect their business.

Concerns about sustainability and the health of the planet are only accelerating, and cannot be ignored by business leaders – and yet, how to define the task and where to start can pose its own challenges. To understand the scope and scale of the task, we need only to listen to a recent comment from one senior leader, 'When we first started talking about becoming more sustainable, we thought it just required putting recycling bins around the place and encouraging people to turn off lights. But the more we began talking about what it meant to us as a community, we realized it was about our values.' Leaders need to define the reach of the sustainability they intend to tackle. Is it the organization's ability to continue as a separate institution at stake? Is the larger ecosystem of stakeholders of which it is a part being fully considered in the company's sustainability strategy? Should the term 'sustainability' take into account the social issues strategy now key to an organization's survival?

Leading sustainability-focused organizational goals goes beyond 'greenwashing' and involves tough calls and challenges on what the business stands for, and what it needs to let go. However, just as it represents more 'hassle and headache' for some leaders, the more enlightened will appreciate that sustainability-focused change can galvanize people to work together in ways that pool energy and innovation. For those organizations going beyond greenwash, the sustainability agenda provides an important new area of focus for harnessing the creativity, commitment and passion of its people.

Leaders are increasingly aware that they need to develop the knowledge, skills and perspective to understand and address these environmental and social challenges, and build companies that meet the needs of society while delivering economic returns to shareholders and stakeholders. Leaders will need to better understand how to reduce risk, create competitive advantage and develop innovative services, products and processes in a sustainable way that builds value for society and protects the planet.

Societal demands for business to play a more responsible role beyond profit

Linked to concerns on sustainability and global warming, and in line with the millennial generation coming of age, the broader societal demands and expectations of business leaders have changed irreversibly. The role of business leaders in society is coming under more scrutiny. Negative external effects like the climate crisis are increasingly visible, automation is sparking fear about the future of work, trust in technology is falling and the most successful companies are becoming more powerful. Leaders are pressed with ensuring that the business creates social as well as economic value. Not only can this increase a company's financial performance in the long run, but it can strengthen the social contract between the business and society, ensuring that the relationship is able to endure.

Five years ago, it was considered good if a company simply did not harm the environment. However, times have changed and now employees demand that their company do more than just not be bad. They need to do good, too. Your company strategy is no longer just about choosing a unique position and doing things differently from competitors – it also has to incorporate the company's relationship to society as readily as to its relationship to its customers and rivals.

Since businesses have the greatest potential to improve the health of our planet and citizens, as they become prosperous, it follows that they are being tasked with a moral obligation to improve the conditions of a system that has helped them succeed. We are beginning to see an evolution in capitalism, from a 20th-century view that the purpose of business is to maximize value for shareholders to a shared view that the purpose of business is to maximize value for society.

Significantly, this transition is being driven not by government regulation, institutional blame or partisanship, but by market-based activism and personal responsibility. We are witnessing an historical moment when, rather than simply debating the role of government in the economy or the role of business in society, people are taking action to harness the power of business to solve society's greatest challenges. This reflects a major culture shift. Business – what we create, where we work, where we shop, what we buy, who we invest in – has become a source of identity, purpose and power.

Leaders are required to respond to this shift, while still playing by the in-house rule book that profit is king. It's a very difficult position for the company's leaders to hold, and something has eventually got to give.

How to set priorities in face of overwhelm, relentless change and uncertainty

In the face of all this relentless change and pressure, priorities keep changing – which is confusing for everyone. The word 'priority' is fast losing its currency when everything seems urgent and important to get done. The landscape keeps shifting, so we have to keep resetting priorities – right? Or are we too much in the detail, so relentlessly buffeted by challenges and events that we have stopped looking at the bigger picture – and this is why we keep setting and resetting priorities and feel so out of control.

I am sure you know the experience of getting up for work in the morning with the feeling of having so much to do that you don't know where to start. It is quite paralysing. When everything that you have to do seems like a priority, it is very tough to figure out where to begin. While we like to set priorities for our tasks, we often forget what's really important. When we are flooded by constant change, it can be easy to lose sight of our true destination. We get derailed and stuck on solving issues, one at a time, instead of remembering to step back and refocus on the outcomes we want to achieve, and prioritizing accordingly how to get there. In the face of relentless change and uncertainty in today's climate, it is a super-important discipline for leaders to be able to stay centred and grounded on what they want to ultimately achieve versus being knocked sideways by the latest issue of the day.

The word 'priority' is fast losing its currency when everything seems urgent and important to get done.

Leaders are at a breaking point, and only the most adaptable will survive

It is not the strongest of the species that survives, not the most intelligent that survives. It is the one that is the most adaptable to change...

CHARLES DARWIN – FUTURE SHAPER

There is too much going on and we are all running too fast. Can this pace be sustained, without reaching some kind of leadership breaking point? Perhaps we are already at the breaking point and only a certain type of leader will survive into the future. This is the premise behind why I am writing this book – what I can offer to you, to help you survive and thrive into the future as a leader in this very challenging world and business environment.

Be assured that while the challenges may feel enormous, this book is full of optimism and I envision the future as an opportunity for all of us as leaders to bring our people forward to a better world, with better outcomes – and not a future where we are spiralling ever out of control and at the mercy of external events. Rather than complain that we, as leaders, face an impossible task, I want to take a more positive problem-solving approach to how to lead in the now and into the future. Turning what could be a leadership crisis into an opportunity, I want to accept and embrace our complex world as the new normal, and recalibrate the new kinds of leadership skills and approaches needed for the now and for the next ten or more years.

This book investigates the types of leadership skills and approach you need in your arsenal to cope with the constant threats, and to lead through disruption, uncertainty and complexity. The emphasis of this book is that it responds directly to the central leadership challenge, with complexity, disruption, AI and digital as its context. This book directly addresses you, the leader reader – first to empathize with the complexity of your day-to-day leadership challenge and secondly to offer you a perspective and some guidance on the kinds of leadership skills and approach you need to cultivate and apply in order to thrive and succeed at a personal leadership level. At times it may feel as if I am asking more reflective questions than supplying all the answers, but bear with me. There is a lot to think about! Let's embark on this journey together and see what conclusions emerge.

Writing this book has been both a cathartic and a constructive exercise as I have attempted to crystallize and articulate the new type of leadership approach and skills we need to cultivate in our world. I see it as an ideal to work towards. I hope it will help you to reset your leadership approach, hone new skills and fulfil your leadership potential. To start with, we certainly all need to be more resilient and resourceful in the face of this ever-increasing complexity. In the now and in the future, resilience may just be the most important competitive tool available to us at an organizational and personal leadership level. What else do we need to think about, as we map out the solution for survival? Let's start with a rewrite of the rules, and a new playbook for how we approach the task of leadership for the future.

Let's take charge and determine our own future, and collectively we can raise our game and shape a better world. What actions can we take today to determine and shape better outcomes for tomorrow? Rather than be overwhelmed by an array of challenges and limitless possibilities, I outline a guiding approach to how to determine a more positive future for you, for your organization and for the world. Step by step you create and shape the future you desire. The first of those steps is to empower yourself and this is the theme of the next part.

PART TWO

Empower yourself

CHAPTER TWO

Future shaper leadership intelligence playbook

Step back to get perspective and see the bigger picture

In face of all this leadership overwhelm, uncertainty and unpredictability, how do you take back control and lead for success? How do you not only react to events, but also take charge and shape the future you want to create? The central challenge for leaders is not just how to keep up but also how to rise up above the constant overwhelm.

The answer – simple at first – is to step back from the detail and the drama, to get a better perspective and see the bigger picture. To remain effective when overwhelmed, you need to create some distance between you and the challenging situation. This helps you to refocus and clarify what really matters, helps you to separate the issues from the underlying problems and reset priorities. When you are stuck in the detail, you are very busy trying to fix issues and resolve problems. When you create the time and space to step back from the day to day, you are able to think more clearly about what you are really trying to achieve long term and it helps you to reset on what is important and what is urgent to invest time on now, in service of your long-term goals. You realize what issues you simply have to let go of, and not invest time on. Going big picture breaks the spell of anxiety overload and that awful feeling of drowning in the detail. To be a truly effective leader, you need to put a premium on staying grounded and having a calm and clear mind. Unclutter your mind, and it will be easier to see the path forward. Get 'unbusy' to become more successful. There is so much perceived status associated with being busy, and yet the people rushing from here to there, with overcrowded minds and long to-do lists, are not the leaders who are going to be able to see the bigger picture and shape a better future for everyone.

To immediately lift myself out of the detail and go big picture, I find it helpful to remind myself of the longer-term strategic end outcome in mind:

- What really matters here?
- What long-term impact am I trying to have?
- What value am I trying to create, and how can I measure my success?

For me, it all crystallizes into one key question for the future shaper leader about what is the long-term strategic end game you want to achieve, ie what is your preferred future outcome? I call this your 'preferable'. The key to setting priorities is to have a crystal-clear vision of the preferable. Then check relentlessly if the tasks you and your teams engage in, or plan to engage in, are in service of that preferred future outcome. Total clarity on the preferable outcome offers relief, and focuses the time and effort of the leader and team.

Do you feel like I am stating the obvious? And yet, lack of clarity on the desired strategic outcome is the number one prevailing time-waster in organizations and the major stumbling block to leadership success. Every textbook and lecture on leadership starts by explaining the importance of the leader having a bold vision. This is absolutely correct, however most textbooks then fail to emphasize the importance of the leader articulating their vision in terms of the final future outcome to be achieved, and by when. Having an outcome-based vision cements your grand aspiration in a clear objective and end date, and gives it more definition, more clarity, more purpose.

For example, if your leadership vision is 'to change the world', 'to make an impact' or 'to make a difference' then realistically that is so broad as to be rendered virtually meaningless. It means everything and nothing when you are trying to lift yourself up out of the detail of your operational role and set a clear direction for other people. The gap is just too huge! Having too broad a leadership vision for your role is almost the same as having no vision at all. Even a leadership vision more grounded in your role but still too vague, such as 'to improve the customer experience' is too open to such a wide spectrum of interpretation by you and your team. It has no calibration in terms of a strategic end goal or what an improved customer experience might ultimately feel like. Unless it is backed up by a specific end goal, different interpretations may result in disjointed projects and lack of total focus on key initiatives that will really fulfil the vision.

The world is confusing enough. Don't add to the confusion. As a future shaper leader, be crystal clear on what you want to achieve, be ambitious and always start with the end in mind. In my view a great leadership vision offers inspiration about a better future state and is described in terms of a clear future preferable outcome. For example, American President John F Kennedy's audacious vision in the early 1960s was as follows: 'To put a man on the Moon by end of the decade'. Simply stated, it offered total clarity of an audacious vision, described in a simple sentence and in terms of the strategic outcome to be achieved and by when. There is no ambiguity. Its clarity also encompasses the significance of the ambition and what it might take in terms of the skill of the team and the new technologies to be mastered on the journey to delivering the outcome.

So your first play as a future shaper leader is to lift yourself out of the day-to-day operational detail, go big picture, go as big as you wish, and have a clearly articulated vision which is defined as your preferred future strategic outcome, and by when. Identification of the preferable lies as the heart of the future shaper leadership intelligence framework described later on in this chapter. It is the first key fundamental of future shaping. Of course, as you know, the identification of your big-picture leadership preferable is easier said than done! In Part Three of this book I devote a whole chapter to helping you with how to step back, connect with your leadership purpose and then identify your future preferable outcome. I offer ideas and frameworks to help you think about what strategic outcomes really matter to you as a future shaper leader.

Realize you have the power to shape the future

Your future depends on what you do today.

MAHATMA GANDHI – FUTURE SHAPER

Being clear about your ambitions is the first step, but of course simply knowing what you want to achieve will not be enough. As well as being crystal clear about the strategic outcome you are trying to achieve, you need to take action in order to convert your preferable into a more predictable outcome by stacking the decks in your favour. The actions you choose to take now can alter and shape what happens next. As well as Gandhi's quote, be inspired by the words of US President Abraham Lincoln, who said 'the most reliable way to predict the future is to create it'! In other words, in the context of all possible futures, if you choose your preferred outcome and stack the deck in your favour, you can convert it into a more predictable outcome. By focusing leadership attention, investment, skill and resources on preferable outcomes, we can shape our own future – or at the very least, increase the likelihood of that particular future occurring. Identify what you want to happen and then put your leadership and team energy, budget, skill and resources into making it happen. The essential role of the future shaper is to convert the preferable into a predictable, ie a more predicted outcome.

The actions you choose to take now can alter and shape what happens next.

In the next part (Part Three) I describe how to establish your preferable future outcome and the further four key future shaper fundamentals you can leverage to manifest the outcome you desire:

- Persuasion: how to convince people to follow you.
- Persistence: how to be resilient and stay the course.
- Prove: how to nurture successful teams and deliver great results.
- Platform: how to power up your network and multiply your impact.

In a nutshell: if you are clear about the future outcomes you want to achieve; and you persuade others to support and resource them; and you are persistent and steadfast in the face of any obstacles; and you nurture winning teams who prove great results; and you grow your network and platform of power – then the future you desire is more likely to be achieved. After a thorough explanation in Part Three of the five future shaper fundamentals (the 'what' you need to do), I devote Part Four to the new future shaper leadership traits you need to cultivate (the 'how') in order to execute the fundamentals. I call this total approach 'future shaping intelligence' and it is my empowering message to you on how to rise above today's overwhelm and lead in an uncertain world.

The future shaper intelligence framework and approach is rooted in the belief that the actions you take today have consequences that affect a future outcome. In other words, follow the approach and you can shape the future outcome you desire. If you want something to happen, fix your aim and take the first step and the next and the next – often referred to as the law of cause and effect. A simple example of the law of cause and effect is 'because I did not set the alarm, I was late for work'. For a business example, try 'I made no effort on business development, and I did not make my sales targets'. Or, more positively, 'I persisted in making calls and I won new business'. Simply put, do something, something will happen or do nothing, nothing will happen. Of course, sometimes, doing nothing is a definite choice, and if that is the case, then do nothing with intent. In physics, the law of cause and effect is described as follows: 'for every action, there is an equal and opposite reaction'. Essentially it is a universal law, which specifically states that every single action in the universe produces a result, no matter what. Every single action you take will have a consequence – 'good' or 'bad'. We know this to be true using our personal experience. This is comforting because it means the leadership decisions you make and the actions you take all matter and nothing is wasted. This law of cause and effect means that you have more power than you realize to shape the future you desire. You can take steps towards your desired outcomes, and realize your goals. It means that you are only at the mercy of events if you decide your only power is to react to what is happening, rather than set out a train of events to create new happenings.

When you fix your goals, and remain steadfast on your mission, you have personal experience of achieving successful outcomes. Remember that promotion you always wanted, you worked hard for, and eventually achieved?! Perhaps it was not all smooth sailing but you got there in the end. Curveballs are less likely to knock us sideways if we are channeling all our focus and energy in a particular direction. Of course, we get knocked down, or knocked sideways at times, but we persevere and get back up again and keep going. Here come cause and effect again. When obstacles knock us, if we get back up we have a fresh shot at achieving the outcome we want. If we stay down, we don't. Don't leave things to chance, don't let others dictate your path – empower yourself. Take action now in pursuit of your goals.

Popular psychology author, Malcolm Gladwell (2008), wrote about the '10,000-Hour Rule' and this is a good example of the law of cause and effect. The 10,000-Hour Rule holds that 10,000 hours of deliberate practice will result in a person becoming world-class in their field. Gladwell puts forward the idea that practising a specific task is the key to success and that can be accomplished with 20 hours of work a week for 10 years. To support his thesis, he cites the examples of sports players, the Beatles and Microsoft co-founder Bill Gates. Bill Gates had rare access to a computer in 1968 at the age of 13, at a time when most of his school friends in Seattle would have been playing basketball. He spent night times and weekends with friends in the computer room, which gave him a substantial head start in the area of programming, and allowed him to build his company at a much younger age than he might otherwise have been able to. Of course, this rule has its detractors and people love to dispute the concept – but you get the idea, it makes logical and intuitive sense. If you dedicate your focus and time towards a future outcome, it follows that you are more likely to get an exceptional result. Energy in equals energy out.

Stop feeling afraid of unknowns and 'wildcard' events

What about external events and obstacles outside our control? Surely we can't just fix our aim, march on and persist no matter what? When the world is evolving at a rapid pace, don't we just need to get better at reacting and responding to the immediate threats presented? Frankly speaking, this is your choice. You can decide you are at the mercy of events and externalities out of your control – and continue to feel powerless and afraid – and it becomes a self-fulfilling negative prophecy. Or you can choose not to be afraid, to embrace change and take action to pursue your goals. How do you choose to invest your emotional energy? Do you want to fear the future or trust in your own capability to shape it?

It might help to analyse what we mean by 'the future', in order to understand it better and be less afraid about what is going to happen next. We don't often think about the future in analytical terms. We usually think about it in very macro and conceptual terms – and increasingly in today's business climate, we think of it fearfully as a state that seems more and more out of our control. So let's break it down and conduct a more rational sense-check of what may or may not be making us fearful and what may or may not be within our control.

The way I like to describe it is that the future is made up of possibles, preferables, predictables and wildcards:

- Possibles: what might happen.
- Preferables: what we want to happen.
- Predictables: what will likely happen.
- Wildcards: total unknowns/unpredictables.

Using trends and forecasting techniques, and our own intuition and experience, we do have a sense of what is possible in the future. As leaders, innovators and entrepreneurs we quite like discussing possibilities and it helps feed our ideas on our preferables. The preferables are the possibilities that we want to manifest. As a general observation on the state of play in leadership and business today, we are not afraid of what is possible: on the contrary we like to embrace it. After all, the possibilities are about future revenue streams via new products and services. Everyone is on disruption alert so fair warning has been given to leaders about investing in innovation, staying in tune with changing consumer needs, staying alert to early seeds of potential disruption and staying ahead on what is possible. The future shaper leader is not afraid of what is possible; possibilities are simply business opportunities waiting to happen.

The predictables are already just about to happen, or with enough support and leverage, we can make them happen. So, predictables shouldn't scare us either. They are already known. We have something of a handle on them, and can make advance plans on how to deal with them.

So that just leaves one aspect of the future, which I guess is the truly scary part for businesses and leaders – the 'wildcards', ie what we can't predict, what we didn't know would be possible, and what are definitely not our preferables. Of course, it is true that we cannot control the true wildcards. There will always be total unknowns and unpredictables in our future. But how scared should we be? In today's volatile world, it feels like there are more wildcards and unpredictables than ever before – but perhaps this is a misperception. Perhaps a significant part of that issue is that we have lost some of our foresight on predicting what could happen next. Perhaps a lack of perspective, a lack of insight and the speed of change has unbalanced us and makes us feel that there are more wildcards – but in reality we just need to get better at reading the early signals, and anticipating the subsequent happenings.

In truth, real wildcards are low-probability and high-impact events. One of the most often cited examples of a wildcard event in recent history is the terrorist attack of 9/11 in New York. Nothing had happened in the past that could point to such a possibility and yet it had a huge impact ever since on everyday life in the United States, and beyond, from simple tasks like how to pack your suitcase for air travel to deeper cultural effects and international affairs. In politics the rise of populism – while feeling shockingly 'wildcard' to begin with, is now being rationalized and explained as an understandable outcome of the disconnect between the elite and the ordinary voter jaded by the current political system. The wildcards may seem wildly unexpected at first, but the smarter we get at reading the signs and anticipating the future, the better we can equip ourselves to anticipate and predict these happenings. Then these events become more predictable, and we can plan in advance. The fear factor can be reduced as we realize that many of these events are not so wild after all. For example, people have been predicting the demise of the high street and the shakeout of the retail landscape since the emergence of internet shopping in the mid to late 1990s so why do we continue to be 'surprised' by any 'breaking news' when a major department store goes bust or shuts down half its bricks and mortar operations. These are not unpredictable events, so let's not confuse an inevitably predictable changing landscape with imagined wildcards and volatility. We knew it was coming and we shouldn't be afraid, we should have planned for it.

Yes, there is an accelerated pace of change in the world today, which presents itself as volatility – and yes, due to technological advances, the rate of change in the future will never be as slow as it is now. But don't be afraid. Fear is the most unhelpful and paralysing emotion of all. It unbalances good leadership decision making, it makes you lose perspective. Take the emotion of fear out of your leadership life, and just get better at investing attention in observing what is happening around you, and your customer. Get better at understanding the possibilities and get better at predicting future outcomes and shaping the preferables you want to see manifest.

Empower yourself to lead; don't wait for permission or the right job title

Another critical element of the future shaper leadership intelligence playbook is to truly empower yourself as a future shaper leader to set the agenda. Don't wait for permission or the right job title to be a future shaper leader. Instead, empower yourself to step up and start making really great decisions about future outcomes, and galvanize others to follow you to achieve the results you desire. Be the creator and shaper of events. Decide what future outcomes you want to achieve, and inspire others to follow you and invest in your ideas, and support you to achieve your goals.

People are assigned the title of 'leader' but it doesn't calibrate how good they are in the position.

If you already have a leadership title, check whether you are taking full advantage of the opportunity as a future shaper. The word 'leader' always reminds me of the word 'parent'. Just because you have children, you are called a parent but it doesn't mean you are a good one. It is the same with the word 'leader'. People are assigned the title of 'leader' but it doesn't calibrate how good they are in the position. In reality, many leaders are still managers who have not yet made the transition to leadership, despite their role title. For example, are you still just following a set of instructions from your boss and relying on the authority of your position to get things done? If that is the case, then you are still just a manager – with a leadership title. Your business performance targets are not the same as having a vision. The overall company business targets do not constitute a leadership vision. Targets and vision are NOT the same thing. Targets, when achieved, are the evidential results that show your vision is on track. Achieving targets that are not contextualized in a big-picture vision that you believe in show you up as merely an instruction taker. Without a bigger-picture vision of the future and a motivated followership, you are not performing a true leadership role.

Unfortunately, in an attempt to manage uncertainty, ambiguity and any overwhelm, our first reaction in our role is to take instructions, to get busy organizing, managing and controlling – instead of rising above the issues and focusing on changing or sustaining the strategic direction and longer-term market success.

Large corporates often have institutional ways of working, stuck cultures, bureaucracy, a complex matrix structure and an overall weight of complexity that is just hard to function within. There is always a temptation for those of us at the top to slip into or be forced into behaving like a professional manager – an 'uber-administrator' – rather than a true leader. It doesn't help that the business is managed quarterly, and there can be massive pressure to hit targets on time and on budget. Inevitably this leads to short-term thinking and suboptimal behaviours. Sometimes it can feel as if all our efforts are in service of the quarterly results rather than the longer-term vision and goals. It is that constant push and pull from serving the long-term vision to hitting our quarterly targets that should make our roles exciting and commercial and relevant – but that juxtaposition brings its own jeopardy to whether we are supposed to be managing or leading or both.

In my experience, we all have the managing part of our role down pat. What we need to get better at is the leadership skills side of our roles. Ask yourself, do you have a tendency towards too much managing and not enough leading?

So, not only do we need to consciously upgrade our leadership skills and approach to become great future shaper leaders, but we also need to start from a position of awareness that we tend to invest too much time on managing instead of leading. This clarity on the baseline makes way for a significant leap in future shaping leadership skills and quality during our future shaper leadership intelligence upgrade.

Most organizations have plenty of great managers. What organizations need now, to succeed in today's world and into the future, are great leaders. I want you to ask yourself what you want to be – a great manager or a great leader? If it is the latter, then give yourself permission right now to step up and commit to being a great future shaper leader. 'Commit' is the critical action word here because it means you agree to invest in yourself and educate yourself on what future shaper leadership really

TABLE 2.1   From managing to leading

From managing ...	...to leading
Guided by short-term targets	Guided by long-term vision
Emphasis on how things are, and exercising tight control over resources	Emphasis on how things could be, and higher appetite for risk and pushing boundaries
I am the expert, and when I get involved I make the difference	I deliver great results by empowering my team members to deliver
My focus is my team and building loyalty	I create networks, beyond my team
I have plenty of experience. I am happy as I am	I am a learner, always seeking to evolve and improve myself
If I work hard, I will be promoted	I take responsibility for creating my own future

means and deliver on this approach in your role. Becoming a future shaper leader won't simply happen – you have to work at it – and this book provides you with a blueprint to follow to make a successful transition.

Apply a new leadership intelligence framework and cultivate more relevant traits

Having set out the case for why we need to evolve our leadership approach, what is the best way forward? Why do we even attempt to package up the complexity of leadership into a neat framework? Well, we do it because a framework is a useful way to make the complexity of leadership simpler. It references the key aspects, and helps guide us on our journey. Of course, in reality, life and leadership is not a linear process and cannot be reduced to a simple set of steps or framework. However, there is still great merit in deconstructing leadership into a framework to help us find a common definition of the critical elements – and to enhance our understanding of important process steps. It means we can coalesce on a useful approach both in the discussion, debate and doing of great leadership, and in the training of ourselves and others on how to action future shaper leadership.

The future shaper leadership intelligence framework is a distillation of how to approach your leadership task as a future shaper. It is about setting a clear direction, bringing people with you and achieving the right results. It centres on the key task of the future shaper, which is to identify your preferables and convert them into predictables. The approach is outcome driven, from the start. As a memory aid, I have organized the future shaper fundamentals around five Ps: preferables, persuade, persist, prove and platform. In the next part, I devote a full chapter to each one. In each chapter, I provide you with a description of the central tenet, and equip you with useful models and examples to help you explore the topic in more detail. I want you to become more aware of the process elements of the leadership framework and to feel more equipped and inspired to apply the learning to your context each time you identify as being involved with each element.

Realize that you have more power than you think

The future shaper leadership intelligence framework also illustrates the wrap-around traits that you will need to cultivate to execute the fundamentals, in order to survive and thrive in today's uncertain and unpredictable world. This is not just about coping with the overwhelm – it is much more than that. It is about stepping up and really taking charge of your leadership role and feeling empowered to shape the future. It is an empowering insight to realize that you have more power than you think and you can take steps now to proactively shape future outcomes.

The framework is an artificial simplification but it is very useful because it forces you to think about each leadership process step more deliberately – starting with what you are actually trying to achieve. Although a leadership process that starts with what you want to achieve may sound like stating the obvious, many so-called leaders would be completely stumped if you asked them to describe to you in one sentence 'what is your leadership vision?' or 'what key long-term strategic outcome are you trying to achieve?' Worse still, if you asked each member of their team the same question, you may get as many different answers as team members. You might be told about their agreed sales targets, due in by end of the fiscal year. But, as I will never tire of pointing out, a set of business targets is not a leadership vision. It is this gap in imagination and understanding between what a long-term strategic vision is and what a year-end business target is that separates the so-called leaders ('instruction

FIGURE 2.1   Future shaper leadership intelligence framework

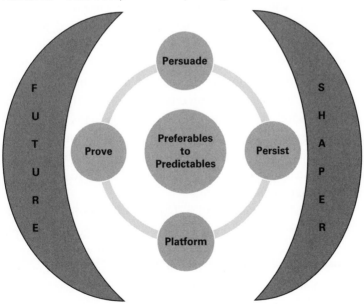

takers') from the visionary leaders ('future shapers'). It's a critical point for future shapers to be very clear on the better future state that they envision and want to aim for. So, the future shaper leadership framework starts right there – and later on I challenge and guide you to think deeply about your leadership purpose, your imagination on what is possible in the future and how to hone in on very specific and clear preferable future outcomes to be achieved.

The central task of the future shaper leader is to identify a clear preferred future outcome, and convert that preferable into a predictable – using the further four key levers of persuade, persist, prove and platform, and by cultivating a new set of relevant future shaper leadership traits.

The future shaping framework acknowledges that leadership is not a solo act – and that the next process step is to galvanize followership to support the achievement of your preferable. Of course, by definition you cannot be a leader without followers, but I don't mean only your team – who may feel more or less obliged to do your bidding – I mean the challenge of persuading key influencers and decision makers to support and resource your preferable. Having set out your preferable outcomes, and persuaded others to back you, the next key process step is about your developing personal resilience and not giving up on your dream of a future better outcome. Easier said than done in today's climate! Finally, the framework highlights the importance of creating a more powerful platform for yourself so that your path to achieving future outcomes is made smoother by having created better networks, access and reach to people and resources that can support you.

Understanding the key future shaper leadership fundamentals is a great place to start, but even with this knowledge many people will still fail. Success does not happen because of what you know. It happens because of the person you become – so understand the fundamentals, practise their application, but also get ready to hear my advice in Part Three on the essential personal leadership traits you will need to cultivate to support you to become the kind of leadership person who can successfully apply the levers. These traits are the wrap-around must-have traits for the future shaping framework to really come to life. Think of these traits as a premium upgrade on traditional leadership skills – a conscious leadership genetic code upgrade, in the face of all that currently threatens us. In the face of all the world and business complexity and uncertainty, are we as leaders going to retrench, batten down the hatches, and apply tried and tested approaches in the hope that our current skills stay relevant and we can weather the storm? Or do we rise up to the challenge, accept disruption as the new normal, and realize that we also need to disrupt our outdated thinking on the types of traits required for great leadership?

In Part Four, I make recommendations on the new set of traits that you should aspire to incorporate into your new leadership genetic code. They are the new building blocks necessary to make the transformation from just-about-coping leader to future shaper leader. Table 2.2 is my list of 12 guiding future shaper traits to help guide you in the bold project of arriving at the kind of impressive leadership we need now; and lay the foundation necessary to successfully apply the future shaper intelligence fundamentals. To help you remember, I have used the acronym F.U.T.U.R.E. S.H.A.P.E.R. to describe the list of traits you need as a future shaper leader.

TABLE 2.2   F.U.T.U.R.E. S.H.A.P.E.R. – future shaper leadership intelligence traits

F	Fearless	**S**	Super-adaptable
U	Unconventional	**H**	Hard-working
T	Tenacious	**A**	Authentic
U	Unifying	**P**	Persuasive
R	Resilient	**E**	Energizing
E	Empathetic	**R**	Resourceful

I call these the genetic code or building blocks of leadership that you need to cultivate to help you to apply the future shaper fundamentals. No point in having a great methodology or approach if you don't have the traits, qualities and characteristics to see you through applying the formula. Your genetic code is not set in stone at birth. Researchers are now discovering that it responds dynamically to your environment, education, thoughts and beliefs. Therefore, it is absolutely possible to upgrade your leadership genetic code through greater self-awareness, better education and more conscious cultivation of your core traits.

As a final point for now on the framework, it is worth noting that it is also very useful as a leadership communications alignment device. I had a recent experience of launching a new team and strategy and suddenly realized we had no common leadership process approach, language or templates to help us articulate and set out what we wanted to achieve. This really brought home to me the gap between a useful leadership framework and process steps, and the usefulness of having a shared methodology so that we can align on a common language and common approach, and more quickly set about achieving our desired outcomes.

Let us move on now to a more detailed examination of the components of the future shaper leadership intelligence framework.

PART THREE

Five key fundamentals of future shaping leadership intelligence

CHAPTER THREE

Preferable: establish your preferred future outcome

The first and critical element of future shaper leadership is to clearly set out the future outcome you want to achieve. However, you need to start with understanding your leadership purpose and motivation before you identify the outcome – because just having the goal is not enough. You require immense drive and a burning desire to achieve it so that when you get to the tricky implementation part, you have the motivation to keep going. Ideas on outcomes are 'cheap' at one level. The hard part is having the intrinsic passion and motivation and skill to go beyond the seed of your idea and implement it. Implementation of change and innovation is what separates the would-be leaders from the real future shaper leaders amongst us.

There are three key aspects to how you establish your preferred future outcome:

- Imperative – understand your purpose and what is motivating you to act now.

- Imagine – explore all the ideas and possibilities.
- Identify – decide on the long-term strategic outcome you want to achieve.

In the section on imperative, I explore the idea of what you want your leadership legacy to be – and how you can reframe your leadership role so that you can reach for ambitious ideas now and be bothered to do what it takes. Without a compelling purpose and reason to act now, even the best idea will languish when faced with first hurdles and opposition. It is all too tempting to procrastinate – not because you are lazy, but because it is so hard to really affect and lead change in organizations where, despite protestations to the contrary, people are largely satisfied, and incentivized, with sticking with the status quo and achieving short-term targets.

Having understood what is intrinsically driving you, the next stage is to imagine and explore all the ideas and possibilities in terms of where you want to place your leadership bets. It is good to consider plenty of options until something really connects, and before you zone in on your key preferable. Go big and go wide first, and then decide on the long-term strategic outcome you want to achieve and what you will focus your leadership time and energy on. For example, US President JFK considered a range of alternative inspiring possibilities, before deciding on sending a man to the Moon. His context and his imperative was an observation that the US needed a unifying event, something that was big and bold and reminded the US people of its potential for greatness.

Imperative – understand your purpose and what is motivating you to act now

Future shaper leadership starts with having a clear vision on the impact you want to make, fuelled by a determination and drive to act now and see out the journey to its rightful conclusion.

This determination and drive is what I refer to as your 'imperative', ie your leadership call to action. Having a great vision of what the future could look like is not enough. Future shaping is about transforming your vision into real impacts – so you need a deep intrinsic imperative to act on your insight and stay the course. Otherwise your vision just remains as a wish or an idea you once had and a dream unfulfilled.

You need to know what outcomes you want to achieve – and *why*, and why is there any *urgency* to act now. If you want to make an impact as a future shaper you need a core intrinsic motivation to think big, to be ambitious with your future outcomes – and to keep yourself and others moving forward relentlessly in spite of any challenge and pushback. The 'why' is commonly referred to as your leadership purpose. Your leadership purpose is your meaningfulness – what you are driven to achieve as a leader. It is your passion, your inner music, your personal inspiration, your reason to get up and go to work in the morning – it is your call to action. Your leadership purpose should be so personally exciting that it acts as a meaningful compass and guide for your leadership journey throughout your whole career – a basis for consistency in your decision making and a clarity on what really matters. It helps you to find fulfilment at work, and to achieve your leadership potential and make an impact.

You need to know what outcomes you want to achieve – and why, and why is there any urgency to act now.

When we understand and align with our purpose, we unlock access to a seemingly unlimited amount of inner energy and motivation to do whatever it takes to ensure we achieve our goals. You can't put a price on the acceleration and uplift in performance that a meaningful purpose will give to your leadership efforts. In the face of relentless challenges and pace of change, the future shaper leader needs to be able to access this type of reserve and source of continuous inspiration, drive and motivation – so understanding your purpose is a critical component of the future shaper make up. However, having purpose is still not enough. You need to have an imperative to act – a burning platform, an urgency – otherwise why bother *now*? You can have a leadership purpose and a leadership vision about a desired future outcome – but no real urgency to act yet. So I want to take this idea of purpose one step further, and say that you also need an imperative – a compelling reason to act now. It could be because you feel so passionate about a cause or new technology, or how to fix your organization – or even society! – or you just want to prove yourself.

Your leadership imperative is about 'Why bother to act – now? What is driving you – now?' – as in why do you want to lead? Why are you in business? Why do you work so hard? Why does your vision of the future really matter? Having a strong imperative to act will motivate you to keep moving forward, to overcome obstacles and fulfil ambitions that, without an intrinsic drive, seem like too much effort or even make it too hard to take the first step. People are inspired by a leader with a strong drive and imperative, so not only does a strong purpose-driven approach fuel you, it also energizes others to follow:

- What is your leadership purpose?
- Why do you care?
- Why do you feel compelled to act now?
- What are the risks of doing nothing?

You might be wondering what all this has got to do with your day job and all the macro issues of leadership overwhelm raised earlier on. Well, step back from your day job for just a minute and try to get more clarity on what you are actually trying to achieve as a leader, and why, and why now. The more crystal clear you are on what you really want to achieve at big picture level, the more you can tune out the noise, the more you can ignore investment of time and energy on unrelated meetings and activities, and the more you can truly focus your mind and attention and the resources of your team on the true mission. This total focus on making the future happen enables you as a leader to elevate yourself out of the day to day and next-quarter targets, to become clearer on the longer-term goals. You become more adept at considering the bigger picture before making important strategic decisions.

Let's take a moment to reflect on what you really, really care about. Of course, we all need to earn an income, and many of us enjoy the status, perks and stimulation of our work day to day. Perhaps you are just fuelled by ambition to succeed – to get your next promotion and climb the career ladder. But let's go a bit deeper now to think about your leadership purpose and what you really care about:

· What are your core values? What do you believe in?
· What are your passions and interests?
· What brings you joy?
· When do you feel most fulfilled at work, outside work?
· Who inspires you?

Reflect on the lasting impact and leadership legacy you want to leave behind. Instead of just considering your leadership career from the narrow perspective of today and your next promotion prospects, let's expand your thinking by looking at the question of leadership career, from the point of view of looking back after retiring. When you are 100 years old, and look back on your life, what is the lasting leadership impact you want to have left behind? This kind of reframe elevates the context from the personal to beyond the self, towards a more global community perspective. In other words, rather than a narrow concept of personal advantage regarding what kind of career and enjoyment you could pursue, think about a broader look back over what impact your leadership life may have had on others and on the world. Shift your perspective from self to legacy impact on others.

FIGURE 3.1 What will be your leadership legacy?

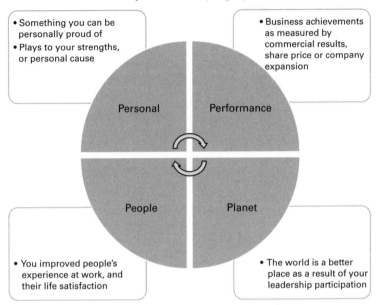

What kind of leadership legacy idea are you drawn towards?

- **Perhaps your legacy will be very 'personal'**
  This could be about something that is a very personal cause of
  yours or very aligned to your unique personal strengths and
  passions as a leader. For example, if you have a strong personal
  cause and want this to be your legacy, perhaps your imperative
  as a female leader becomes 'To champion the inclusion of
  women in business' or similar, that speaks to your personal
  context and passions.
- **Perhaps your legacy will be more about 'performance'**
  A legacy about performance is about having the satisfaction of
  building new businesses and leaving behind lasting commercial
  results and a more robust company. For example, if you love
  building businesses and you want this to be your legacy to the
  world, then perhaps your imperative now becomes 'To create

a $1 billion dollar company' or similar, that speaks to your performance ambitions.

- **Perhaps your legacy will be more about 'people'**
  A legacy about people is about your drive to improve the lives of others. You may have particular interests in shaping the next generation of leaders or improving the working conditions or work–life balance of your teams. For example, if a leadership legacy around making a difference to the lives of others really inspires you, then perhaps your imperative now is 'To improve the lives of other people'.
- **Perhaps your legacy will be more focused on 'planet'**
  This is all about making the world a better place. You may want to make improving the environment your central mission – and that may become about harnessing new technologies to reduce wasteful exploitation of the earth's natural resources or about discovering alternative energy supplies. For example, if it is our environment that is your passion, then perhaps your imperative now becomes 'To make a positive impact on the environment'.

Of course, your legacy could be one that integrates and links with more than one P and possibly all four. It is helpful to deconstruct the idea of legacy into four component parts to help you to think about what you want your legacy to be, and then the response that emerges may well encompass more than one P.

Don't feel restricted to my framework. Another tip on how to figure out what really matters to you is to seek feedback on how those close to you perceive what you stand for – your partner, friends, parents, close colleagues, children. Ask them to share what they think you stand for and what you seem naturally hard-wired to achieve. Find your own way of exploring and articulating your desired leadership legacy and compelling reason to lead now.

For some, it may be very clear what their leadership legacy and purpose is, and it may be a phrase that has particular personal resonance and meaning. For example, 'I want to make a difference' or 'I want to bring light to every situation', or more role-focused such as 'I want to create more opportunities for customer choice' or 'I want to be a global expert in my industry'. Whatever it is, your leadership purpose must be meaningful to you. Drop any temptation to use jargon, and find a very personal statement that resonates with you. Stretch yourself to define purpose that is as specific as possible. Try to go beyond generalized language and current popular Millennial sentiment such as 'I want to make an impact'.

If the legacy framework seems too high-level for now, start with what you could achieve in your role and organization. Think about the higher purpose of your organization and how you could align to support it – or innovate to come up with new ideas. When you have settled on your leadership purpose then think about why it matters to start to take action on it. Reflect on why it is urgent to act now. If you like the sound of your leadership purpose, but it is not accompanied by any sense of urgency, then go bigger, be more ambitious – stretch your ideas until you find something so personally important and compelling to you that you feel that you have no choice but to do something about it.

EXAMPLES OF WHY IT MAY BE URGENT TO ACT NOW

- Because you are ambitious and want to make fast progress.
- Because of huge risks inherent for you/for your organization/for your team in doing nothing.
- Because you want your next promotion.
- Because you care deeply about the outcome.
- Because your ambition is so huge, and there will be so much to do in your lifetime, that you want to start as soon as possible.

At the end of this exercise, if you feel as if nothing has resonated, and nothing really matters to you, you really need to ask yourself why you don't have an intrinsic driving motivation for achieving big-picture goals. Have you never really given it much thought? Why not? Something must be driving you to get up in the morning and achieve. Try to dig deep and find something more meaningful than just money, power and status, so that you are fuelled by deeper intentions when the going gets tough.

Be assured that some people struggle with defining their leadership purpose and imperative. Some people land on their purpose within minutes, while others agonize over it for months and years. Life is a journey of self-discovery, and as you learn more about yourself, it stands to reason that you will better be able to make sense of your existence on the planet. Although it's a struggle, it will be worth it – we all know how inspiring it is when we see or hear from leaders who radiate a strong purpose and call to action.

Your work is going to fill a large part of your life, and the only way to be truly satisfied is to do what you believe is great work. And the only way to do great work is to love what you do. If you haven't found it yet, keep looking. Don't settle. As with all matters of the heart, you'll know when you find it.

STEVE JOBS – FUTURE SHAPER

As you grow older and wiser, you may refine or change your leadership purpose. At different stages of your life, and as circumstances change your leadership purpose may adjust accordingly. For example, in your 20s you may see your purpose as being more dynamic, such as building a great company that will have a lasting positive impact on the world. Whereas in your 50s, you may see your purpose as giving back and acting more as a business mentor versus business builder.

GRETA THUNBERG – FUTURE SHAPER

Greta Thunberg offers a great example of someone who has combined purpose and imperative in service of achieving her future desired outcome.

The climate crisis has already been solved. We already have all the facts and solutions. All we have to do is to wake up and change.

In her passionate 2018 TED Talk call to action, 16-year-old climate activist Greta Thunberg explains her imperative and why, in August 2018, she walked out of school and organized a strike to raise awareness of global warming, protesting outside the Swedish parliament and grabbing the world's attention.

When I was about eight years old, I first heard about something called climate change or global warming. Apparently, that was something humans had created by our way of living. I was told to turn off the lights to save energy and to recycle paper to save resources. I remember thinking that it was very strange that humans, who are an animal species among others, could be capable of changing the Earth's climate. Because if we were, and if it was really happening, we wouldn't be talking about anything else. As soon as you'd turn on the TV, everything would be about that. Headlines, radio, newspapers, you would never read or hear about anything else, as if there was a world war going on. But no one ever talked about it. If burning fossil fuels was so bad that it threatened our very existence, how could we just continue like before? Why were there no restrictions? Why wasn't it made illegal? To me, that did not add up. It was too unreal…

… especially when it comes to the sustainability crisis, where everyone keeps saying climate change is an existential threat and the most important issue of all, and yet they just carry on like before. I don't understand that, because if the emissions have to stop, then we must stop the emissions. To me that is black or white. There are no gray areas when it comes to survival. Either we go on as a civilization or we don't. We have to change...'

Source: TED Talk transcript, TEDx Stockholm, 2018

Imagine – explore all the ideas and possibilities

The true sign of intelligence is not knowledge, it is imagination.
Imagination is everything. It is the preview of life's
coming attractions.

ALBERT EINSTEIN – FUTURE SHAPER

With the backdrop of your leadership purpose, motivation and urgency in mind, the next step is to unleash the full force of your **imagination** on possible preferred strategic outcomes. For example, if your driving imperative is 'to inspire people to bring their best to work' then how ambitious, how imaginative do you want to be about what that means in reality. How that would manifest in terms of tangible outcome within a set period of time like 10 years or even longer? What results would you have to achieve in the interim to know that you are indeed 'inspiring people'? Would it be about your team doubling the revenue of your business or silo, or about improving the lives of your workforce, or about you and your team developing new products and services or cracking the code on cryogenics – what is it about?

Ideate first, without limits - and later on you can figure out the how.

The best way to ideate on the preferable outcome is to deliberately and temporarily suspend immediate concerns on how to do it. Ideate first, without limits, and later on you can figure out the how. This approach offers tremendous freedom to imagine any future outcome you like, unfettered by the how – yet. Breakthrough innovative ideas are possible with this approach. For example, driverless cars were first stated as an outcome, and as you know, the mainstream 'how' is still being figured out. Putting a man on the Moon was an ambitious outcome – no one knew how to do it when US President JFK put this desired outcome forward. As well as – temporarily – removing the limitation of the how, when you know the destination, or have a clear picture of what success looks like, it will sharpen your focus, eliminate tasks that add no value, help increase your effectiveness and help you assemble the right kinds of skills required on the team. In President JFK's case, the Apollo team recruitment strategy was not to hire seasoned engineers, but instead to recruit younger engineers. The younger recruits were more idealistic and did not have the baggage of experience that brought with it a mindset that it was not possible to fulfil the mission. A clear outcome helps you to set direction for your team, and with the right team on board, you can empower them to determine the best way to achieve it. The more clearly you can define the desired outcome, the more focused everyone becomes and the more likely you are to achieve your goals.

Once you have a clear future legacy or achievements in mind, now imagine all the possible future outcomes that would manifest your vision. For example, if your imperative is to improve the environment then are you proposing alternative products, processes, systems or approaches? Or do you think about how you can be an influencer on the world stage? Or perhaps you just want to role model small changes in your own team to your wider organization – and create a very positive ripple effect. Or all of the above? If you can convert your imperative into more tangible desired outcomes with a timeline, it means you are closer to defining and shaping the future you want.

Technology and AI are presenting us with a massive array of possibilities for imagining possible futures. If we can imagine it, then it can happen. We talk to the internet, we attempt to terraform Mars, we manipulate gene codes, we enjoy our new wearables and each new stride forward stimulates our imagination further on what is possible. Also, the rapidly reducing cost of developing new technologies is such that cost is no longer a great barrier to innovation. So quickly has AI accelerated from being just automated machine learning, we are already seeing the emergence of humanoid robotics being used as customer service terminals in airports and replica humanoid newsreaders in China.

These are not the sterile experiences we once imagined. Investment in artificial emotional intelligence continues to soar, whereby robots simulate human emotions. If technology and AI are the great enablers, and anything is possible, that leaves us with our imagination and how to fuel it to achieve the future we desire.

Imagination is about being open to limitless possibilities. It is the opposite of a status quo mindset:

- Do you have the imagination for what's possible?
- Can you push past the limits of how things are done today?
- Are you good at spotting gaps and what's missing – in structures, products, processes?

You could just ask customers what they need or want – but you won't always find the next big idea in a focus group. For example

FIGURE 3.2   Fuelling the imagination

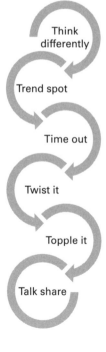

Think differently

Trend spot

Time out

Twist it

Topple it

Talk share

Steve Jobs, former CEO of Apple, came up with the iPad, not because he asked customers what they wanted (after all, they already had the smartphone) but because he spotted the intersection between the traditional laptop and the smartphone – combined with the appreciation of a beautiful aesthetic and a new entertainment device.

Let's think about different ways to fuel your imagination, spot new areas of attention which could shape possible future outcomes:

- Think differently: change how you think, think in pictures, think in metaphors, think differently.
  - Get out of your echo chamber. Find ways to meet people from other cultures/subcultures. Read publications that offer alternative viewpoints. Actively seek out people from diverse and minority backgrounds for your team and listen carefully to their ideas and experiences and different outlook.
- Trend spot: notice the zeitgeist, see what patterns and trends are emerging, keep a close eye on what the customer wants, rather than on what your competitors are doing. Also closely examine the data coming out of your organization – what is the data telling you? What are the insights?
  - Get up to speed on the latest world trends and innovations. Read what the futurist consulting firms are publishing. Pay keen attention to younger generation and what appeals to them.
- Time out: give yourself space to de-crowd your mind, allow yourself to daydream and let ideas come from within.
  - Carve out time in your busy schedule to 'do nothing'. It may be your daily commute or your lunch time; or schedule actual work time for at least 20 minutes to step back and daydream about the bigger picture. Bring your purpose to mind regularly to remind yourself what is driving you and what this is all for. Give yourself some space so that ideas can find you.

- Twist it: look at ideas that work in one context and imagine applying them to another. There may be ideas already manifest in a different geography that can be applied in yours. Or in a different industry, and can be applied in yours. Look at intersections to anticipate what customers may appreciate.
  - Originality and innovation can be achieved by moving an obvious idea from one context and applying it to another. You don't have to pressurize yourself into coming up with brand new ideas. Often there is nothing new, but twisted into a different context the application of the same thing can be perceived as breakthrough in a different geography or industry.
- Topple it: observe the norms in your industry and play with the idea of toppling them. What if the normalized industry drivers were toppled – what could cause this? What would happen next? Be your own disruptor. What would it take to destroy your business?
  - Step outside your organization to examine and explore what is happening with the competition, with other industries, in other countries. Scan the horizon to appreciate trends and to identify or create the disruptors to your industry or business. Design an app that destroys your organization's business model and show it to your boss.
- Talk share: share ideas or the seeds of ideas with others, get their reaction and stimulate more ideas
  - Nurture and stimulate imaginative processes. Be relentlessly curious, seek out new experiences, exposure to new people and the avant garde, enjoying breaking down barriers, pushing boundaries and loving the new.

Use any of the above or any useful methods of your own. Another way to find new ideas is to think about the higher purpose of your organization, and what other ways you might serve that higher purpose (even if it is different from what is done right now):

TABLE 3.1 Ideas based on higher purpose

Company type	Lower-level needs served	Higher-level purpose	Ideas relating to higher-level purpose
Vacation resort	A place for rest, enjoy new food and take a swim	Helping people connect with loved ones	Provide family-support counselling services
Bank	Interest on savings investments	Help people deal with their money wisely	Advisory services on making social-impact investments

Be imaginative about all of the possibilities and then the final step on 'preferable' is to narrow down or zone into identifying the specific future outcome that is your leadership stake in the ground.

Identify – decide on the long-term strategic outcome you want to achieve

Having ideated and imagined a range of possible future outcomes aligned with your leadership imperative, take stock and identify your clear preferred outcome, ie your preferable. Your preferable is narrowed down from the list of possibilities. While you can be as ambitious and imaginative as you like, the final step is to decide the specific strategic outcome you want to achieve. Think of it like throwing a javelin into a future – in terms of your greatest stretch ambition, and where you want to land. Then with that in mind, start with a nearer-term goal, and decide how you show up tomorrow. So, the final step in the 'preferable' element of the future shaper fundamental is about 'identify', which refers to confirming the tangible future outcome you wish to achieve, and by when. Your leadership vision will also need to be grounded back down in your day to day role and targets.

Although, of course, you could set out a number of preferables, I recommend you focus on just one big strategic outcome. When you have one clear preferable you can be more focused now on how you invest your time and energy; you know exactly what you are aiming for, and it crystallizes what is in or out of scope.

When you start with the end in mind in terms of what you want to achieve by when, driven by meaningful purpose you are totally set up for success – you are clear on the destination and you feel motivated to persist if and when any obstacles or challenges arise that have the potential to derail you. Deciding your preferred future outcomes gives you a clear sense of direction. As the well-known quote goes, 'If you don't know where you are going, you might end up someplace else'. If you know what future outcomes you want to achieve, you can align your time, energy and resources in support of achieving those outcomes and this stacks the deck in favour of bringing those future outcomes into reality.

If you have a clear vision, and a strong driving imperative on why this vision is so important to achieve, you will feel inspired to act and you will more easily inspire others to help you to achieve your goals. You are more likely to succeed when you have clear outcomes in mind. You are additionally more likely to succeed when you connect into a meaningful why; you tap into intrinsic motivations and powerful inner resources like resilience and resourcefulness. You will do what it takes to succeed. You are less likely to give up. You will stay the course on creating the future you want and stay steadfast in the face of obstacles.

If you want to be a leader, take a stand and decide what exactly you are going to lead.

Perhaps you are concerned that your preferred vision of the future outcome has nothing to do with your current role requirements, so how do you square that circle? After all, there's no point talking to your boss about changing the world, if all he cares about is that you hit your sales targets? For me, this is a

TABLE 3.2   Confirmation of your future preferred outcome

Imperative →	Imagine →	Identify →	Preferable
What is my leadership purpose? Why do I care? What is my compelling reason to act now? What is the risk of doing nothing?	Brainstorm all the possible big leadership ideas I could focus on – on personal, people, performance, planet, or my role, my organization, my customers, the world.	Make a choice. Narrow down all the possibilities and identify my preferable outcome.	What kind of future outcome do I want to achieve?

crucial point about leadership. If you want to be a leader, take a stand and decide what exactly you are going to lead. If you don't take a stand, accept that you're not a true leader – you are just someone in charge of getting things done. So – to revisit some ground already covered – are you just planning on following instructions? If the answer is yes, then you are a manager, not a true leader. If that's okay with you, no need to read on. You have decided you are not a leader. However, if you truly want to be a leader, then you need to have a vision of a future outcome you want to achieve. Do you have a bigger-picture vision for yourself, your role or your organization? Is there a more ambitious vision for your role and what you can achieve within it? Is there a more ambitious vision for your department, and how can you convince others? Is there a more ambitious vision for your company, your industry, the world – and do you want to lead it?

HENRY FORD – FUTURE SHAPER

Henry Ford is an iconic example of a future shaper who had a clear preferable in mind. His purposeful, imaginative and clear future preferable outcome was to provide affordable mobility to the masses. He cared deeply, which compelled him to act.

I will build a motor car for the great multitude.

Henry Ford is most famous for founding the Ford Motor Company and developing innovative concepts in manufacturing. Ford conceived and introduced the assembly line as a form of mass production in 1914. Although Ford did not invent the automobile or the assembly line, he developed and manufactured the first automobile that many middle-class Americans could afford. In doing so, Ford converted the automobile from an expensive curiosity into a practical conveyance that would profoundly impact the landscape of the 20th century. His introduction of the Model T automobile revolutionized transportation and American industry.

After the birth of the Model T in October 1908, in the first 19 years of the Model T's existence, he sold 15,500,000 of the cars in the United States, almost 1,000,000 more in Canada, and 250,000 in Great Britain, a production total amounting to half the auto output of the world. The motor age arrived owing mostly to Ford's vision of the car as the ordinary man's utility rather than as the rich man's luxury. Once only the rich had travelled freely around the country; now millions could go wherever they pleased. The Model T was the chief instrument of one of the greatest and most rapid changes in the lives of the common people in history, and it effected this change in less than two decades. Farmers were no longer isolated on remote farms. The horse disappeared so rapidly that the transfer of acreage from hay to other crops caused an agricultural revolution. The automobile became the main prop of the American economy and a stimulant to urbanization – cities spread outward, creating suburbs and housing developments – and to the building of the finest highway system in the world.

As the owner of the Ford Motor Company, he became one of the richest and best-known people in the world. He is credited with 'Fordism': mass production of inexpensive goods coupled with high wages for workers. Ford had a global vision, with consumerism as the key to peace. His intense commitment to systematically lowering costs resulted in many technical and business innovations, including a franchise system that put dealerships throughout most of North America and in major cities on six continents. Ford left most of his vast wealth to the Ford Foundation and arranged for his family to control the company permanently.

The man who will use his skill and constructive imagination to see how much he can give for a dollar, instead of how little he can give for a dollar, is bound to succeed.

Henry Ford's business intellect permanently transformed the economic as well as the social character of the United States. Within five years of the inception of Ford Motors, it produced 267,720 cars and employed 13,000 people. Within a decade, he had captured a 48 per cent share of the US car market with $100 million in annual sales.

Sources: www.brainpick.com/people-who-changed-the world in business; https://www.britannica.com/biography/Henry-Ford; www.reference.com/history; www.en.Wikipedia.org

If you have a vision for preferred future outcomes, but it is entirely divorced from how you currently earn your income, then you have some decisions to make. Could you align your role with your preferable by moving role within the company, or by changing company? If you feel truly motivated to action your preferable outcome, you will find a way forward. I remember back when 'corporate social responsibility' (CSR) was emerging as a new idea; some truly motivated individuals persuaded their company bosses to let them set up a CSR unit. Now having a CSR function is the norm and even brand-central. What is your equivalent cause or idea today? And if it is not within your existing role remit, can you convince your company to give you the budget to set it up, to add it as a plus-one to your existing role or incubate something entirely new? 'Persuading' isn't necessarily as simple as it may first sound. It means truly buying into your own vision, and being resourceful about convincing others to buy into your vision.

Of course, it is very hard to achieve something very ambitious on your own. It is not enough to have a strong vision of the future outcomes you want to achieve, driven by personal meaning and passion. The next key step is to persuade others to support you. Now the really hard work on future shaping leadership begins! To convert your preferables into predictables (ie more predictable outcomes) requires support and investment from other people for your ideas. No man is an island – and for sure, no leadership exists without followership. The more followership you have and the better resourced your ideas, the better stacked the odds in your favour of achieving your goals. In the next chapter I take you through three actions you can take to inspire and grow followership for your preferables.

Key takeaways

- If you truly want to be a future shaper leader, it is not just about defining your preferred future outcome, it is about understanding and connecting with the driving force of motivation behind the outcome; the critical question of 'why bother – now?'
- Think about what motivates you as a leader, and what leadership legacy you want to leave behind.
- Unleash your full imagination when thinking about future possible outcomes. Don't worry about the how – yet. Be ambitious.
- Staying ambitious and big-picture, decide on your key preferred strategic outcome, and commit to focusing your leadership attention and skill on its achievement.

CHAPTER FOUR

Persuade: convince people to follow you

The next important element of the future shaper leadership intelligence framework is 'persuade', which is about creating followership and galvanizing others to buy into your preferable. It is unlikely you will be able to deliver an ambitious long-term strategic all outcome on your own, so how do you convince other people to believe in you and what you want to achieve? Even if you are in a strong position of power already, the old model of a leader as an authority figure at the top simply telling people what to do, and letting their diktat cascade down through the management ranks, is no longer realistic. A command and control style of leadership is out, and in its place the future shaper leader needs to mobilize people around a compelling vision of the future. If you work in a complex, matrixed organization, then as you know, getting anything done is all about influence and persuasion.

There are three key aspects to how you convince people to follow you:

- Inspire – communicate your vision and motivate others to follow you.
- Influence – understand the politics and where decision-making power lies.
- Investment – secure resources to build your team and finance your plans.

In this chapter, I offer ideas on how best to communicate your vision and motivate others to follow you. As a future shaper leader, you will best inspire other people by sharing your purpose, and engaging people on the bigger-picture ambition and why they should support you and join you to achieve the desired outcome. You will need to paint a picture for people of what is possible and motivate them to make those possibilities real. To help guide you, I set out a useful structure for how to communicate and pitch your idea to others.

Even if you run your own company, you will not be able to escape strong influencers such as board members, investors or your key customers. To achieve your preferable, you will need to understand the politics and where decision-making power lies. I offer you strategies for identifying who to influence and how. For example, it will be much easier to gather support for your preferable if you have already nurtured the relationship with the key people who matter in the decision. If you are politically astute, you will be better equipped to anticipate stakeholder concerns and agendas, and find ways to align all agendas for the highest good. Finally, you really only know you are successful at persuasion when you secure the people resources and financial backing you need. So in this chapter I also address how to secure resources to build your team and finance your plans.

Inspire – communicate your vision and motivate others to follow you

In the 1980s and 1990s and certainly in the decades prior, the business leaders sat at the top table, issuing edicts and instructions. Employees did what they were told, more or less, without any pushback or challenging why. That approach doesn't cut it anymore. Today's workforce is more empowered and more educated, more self-directed and more demanding. Traditional corporate hierarchies have given way to flatter structures, more transparent decision making and more democratic consensus building on the way forward. The most successful leaders have to learn how to inspire, how to influence, and how to engage their people and build followership beyond positional power (ie the authority and influence that comes with a senior role).

To inspire people with your preferable vision of the future, think about who you need to inspire and how to communicate with them to get them involved, to support you in making that future vision a reality. It is not always easy to lift your head above the parapet to speak up and speak out about what you truly believe in. A considerable personal effort may be required – but with a true vision in mind, driven by strong and meaningful purpose, you will be able to motivate yourself to do what it takes. First, make sure you are fully convinced yourself! Unless you truly believe in yourself and your idea, why would anyone else?

My generation were brought up to believe in the virtue of hard work and 'meaningfulness' was rarely, if ever, discussed, neither at the dinner table, nor in the board room! However, time has moved on, and the role of work has changed. All the indicators are that for the millennial generation, meaningfulness at work is the new motivation. So if you want to shape the future, and inspire others to support you, you need to communicate your purpose, your imperative and why your preferable

FIGURE 4.1   Who do you need to convince?

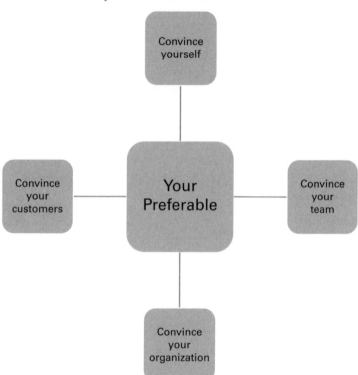

outcome is meaningful; and why it matters – not just to you, but why it should matter to everyone else too. The more you can tap into the passions of other people and align their energy with your preferable, the more you grow your support base and likelihood of achieving the future you want.

When other people are on board, you might need to recalibrate or co-create a new and even more meaningful preferable, better than the one you originally set out. However, there is a difference between collaboration with others that helps build a better vision, and allowing others to overwhelm you and dominate you into changing your ideas. You need to be the guardian of your vision of the future and hold it steadfast if you truly believe in it. It may take a while to convince other people – especially if your ideas are quite radical. Be patient and persevere.

When I think about what kind of person inspires me, I think about someone who is self-assured, confident, passionate, purposeful, who does the right thing, who does not have a selfish agenda, who wants to achieve higher goals and make a difference. There is something very resonant, something very human-to-human to have that kind of connection with someone, whereby you believe in their vision of the future because you believe

Being inspired is like being lifted up to another level of awareness and hope for what might be possible

in them. You decide to follow them, you support their agenda and want to know more, to do more, to learn more about it. Being inspired is like being lifted up to another level of awareness and hope for what might be possible. It takes us out of our day-to-day status quo and motivates us to do more. When I urge you to 'be inspiring!' I am fully aware that this is easier said than done and it is a very tall order for mere mortals like you and me! But we don't have to start with inspiring a nation. Let's start with inspiring one person, and then another, and soon other people will hear the story and will be drawn to it. I call it 'quiet inspiration' because I like the idea of a 'quiet revolution' – ie no outlandish rally cries, no posturing and vain declarations but instead quietly spoken meaningful connections with other people that start out small but may lead to transformational change or difference.

Start with a safe place to practise sharing your idea. Gather one or two of your colleagues together and talk about your preferable. Ask for their honest reactions, listen to their questions. Figure out if you need to reshape and reframe how you articulate your ideas. Very often we have a clear vision in our minds of an end state, but it can take a few iterations before we can properly articulate that to other people, so that they fully understand.

Something that may seem perfectly obvious to you may require a more detailed breakdown when describing it to someone else. Your words may, at first, not fully articulate the meaning of what you want to achieve – it can take practice to find the right words that resonate better with the listener. Sometimes your ideas may be so conceptual that you have to break them down into more tangible examples, drawing on metaphors that can more simply explain something quite complex. Admit it if your argument is not perfect, allow the opinions of others to seep in and be willing to make adjustments if the rigidity of your position is off-putting or unhelpful.

How to inspire and excite people about your preferable

1 PREFERABLE OUTCOME: DESCRIBE THE BIG-PICTURE VISION

- Begin with the big idea and why. Lay out your vision in a concise and clear fashion.
- Clearly define what the world would look like if your vision were to succeed.
- Communicate meaning and hope. Ask inspiring questions such as 'Wouldn't it be great if we could do this for our people? Our industry? Our world?'
- Top tips:
  - Use your words to paint a picture. Research shows that people are far more likely to be persuaded by something they can visualize. Use powerful visual imagery and/or tell vivid stories that breathe life into your ideas. Good storytelling can create inspiring images in the mind of the listener. Identify the mutual/universal benefits of this better future to promote cooperation from others.
  - Use an enthusiastic tone, great eye contact, leaning forward towards the person/people you are talking to. Depending on whether you are trying to persuade your peers or a set of investors, change your approach. For example, the former will more likely want peer-to peer-respect, equal dialogue

and evidence of mutual benefits, whereas the latter are more concerned with robust facts and figures, and information on return on investment timelines.

2 IMPERATIVE: COMMUNICATE THE URGENCY

- Describe the problem – why this vision of the future has not yet come to pass.
- Communicate the issues, obstacles and struggles.
- Explain the urgency and compelling need to take action now.
- Top tips:
  - Be prepared to invest significant time upfront convincing your first followers and it will become easier from there. When you share your ideas, notice and listen to how people respond to you.
  - Try to show a proven example of what is possible: are there examples of what you are trying to achieve already evident in small green shoots elsewhere – in another industry or geography? Or perhaps you can show an example through clever use of metaphor. Have you run a pilot or test case?

3 JOURNEY: OUTLINE WHAT IT WILL TAKE

- Describe what has to happen to achieve our future desired reality.
- Communicate the change necessary.
- Top tips:
  - People resist change unless they can be sure it is worth the pain of the effort or transition so be patient as you explain what you need. Expect pushback, especially if your ideas are quite radical. Use both logic and emotional appeal to explain why the journey is necessary. It will not be enough to use just emotional appeal. Logic appeals to the reasoning power of the person you're trying to persuade (eg since $a + b = c$, and $b + a = d$, surely you can see that d must equal c). Emotion appeals to the emotional ties of the person you're

trying to persuade (eg do this because you believe in me. Do this because you love your children and want the best future for them). Both strategies used together can be very powerful.

4 ENLIST: RALLY SUPPORTERS

- Break down the actions needed for how to do it and the resources needed, and enlist support.
- Communicate the action steps.
- Ask people to join you, to help you, to make introductions, to support you.
- Top tips:
  - Don't overwhelm people with your enthusiasm. Give them a chance to absorb your ideas and give them time to think about how they can support you.

MICHELLE OBAMA – FUTURE SHAPER

Using an example outside of the corporate world, we could look at Michelle Obama as an iconic female leader who is on a purposeful mission to persuade young black women and schoolgirls in economically disadvantaged areas to fulfil their potential. Michelle's future shaping preferable outcome is to help influence the education of the 62 million girls around the world who aren't in school.

I see myself in these girls, I see my daughters in these girls, and I simply cannot walk away from them. And I plan to keep raising my voice on their behalf for the rest of my life. I plan to keep urging world leaders to invest in their potential and create societies that truly value them as human beings. I plan to keep reaching out to local leaders, families, and girls themselves to raise awareness about the power of sending girls to school.

She speaks encouragingly and directly to schoolgirls she meets, using straightforward language; 'If you want to know the reason why I'm standing here, it's because of education... I liked being smart. I loved being on time. I loved getting my work done.

I thought being smart was cooler than anything in the world.' Her ability to connect comes from speaking from the heart and embodying the example of a girl who has much in common with the children she seeks to inspire. She also speaks to the hopes and interests of their educators and influencers:

- *'I am an example of what is possible when girls from the very beginning of their lives are loved and nurtured by people around them. I was surrounded by extraordinary women in my life... who taught me about quiet strength and dignity.'* (Preferable outcome/hope.)

- *'I am so tired of fear. And I don't want my girls to live in a country, in a world, based on fear.'* (Imperative.)

- *'One of the lessons that I grew up with was to always stay true to yourself and never let what somebody else says distract you from your goals. And so when I hear about negative and false attacks, I really don't invest any energy in them, because I know who I am.'* (Journey.)

- *'You may not always have a comfortable life and you will not always be able to solve all of the world's problems at once but don't ever underestimate the importance you can have because history has shown us that courage can be contagious and hope can take on a life of its own.'* (Journey.)

- *'Whether you come from a council estate or a country estate, your success will be determined by your own confidence and fortitude.'* (Enlist.)

Sources: https://obamawhitehouse.archives.gov/letgirlslearn; Obama (2015); https://www.ted.com/talks/michelle_obama/transcript

Influence – understand the politics and where decision-making power lies

Embrace politics, negotiation and lobbying skills as part of your future shaper leadership role. As soon as I mention the word 'politics' people start to groan – or distance themselves from the very act 'I don't do politics', 'I don't like politics', 'I don't believe in politics'. All of which is extremely naïve – especially if you want to move into senior leadership ranks. Wherever there are people, there are politics – and it can be a skill that once understood can be managed for the better of everyone, and not always be aligned with negative connotations. You need to embrace the politics if you want to succeed as a future shaper.

Be politically astute about the hierarchy of influence. You may only need to convince one powerful sponsor or a few key influencers about your preferable, and they might do most of the hard work in persuading others. For example, if you can put your preferable as a priority item on the agenda of the CEO, perhaps you won't need to convince anyone else! If the CEO believes in your idea, you will have access to all his influencers and resources. I appreciate that – however open the communication channels are supposed to be – it is not always easy to get even five minutes with your CEO. See it more like a metaphor and identify key decision-makers and influencers to inspire, who can subsequently galvanize and mobilize their networks. Apart from the CEO, there will be other key influencers in your organization or industry who represent a wider network of people. Being politically astute about the key influencers is an important currency for ensuring you achieve support and resources to secure your preferable outcomes. So let's think about who really matters in terms of support for your ideas.

Wherever there are people, there are politics

It may be relatively easy to influence your team – they already know and trust you, and are more incentivized to please you. It is much harder to convince people outside of your direct line of control. In any case, it can't be just about seeking compliance, about getting people to go along with what you want them to do. You will need genuine commitment from others to accomplish ambitious goals and tasks. True commitment means you have succeeded in inspiring people so that they'll truly endorse and truly support you, even in the face of major setbacks and obstacles. In today's turbulent economy, when you're so often implementing big change, cutting back on resources or dealing with tough challenges, you need all the commitment, or engagement, you can get.

It may be contextual according to the ambition of your preferable, but in general the stakeholder groups you need to energize/influence/inspire will likely fall into one or more of these categories:

- your team;
- your boss;
- your peers;
- your boss's boss;
- the CEO and top leadership team;
- your customers/the public;
- your industry;
- national bodies;
- international organizations.

You may prefer to test out your ideas with your team. However, when thinking about the powerful influencers on this list, in order of ranking, you probably should flip the list from bottom to top. Depending on your network and state of relationships, figure out your point of entry on this list of people to inspire.

Who are the powerful influencers of others?

Ranked in order of influence:

- international organizations;
- national bodies;
- your industry;
- your customers/the public;
- the CEO and top leadership team;
- your boss's boss;
- your peers;

- your boss;
- your team.

Understanding where power levers lie is very important – for fast-tracking your ideas and getting other people on board. If you can impress the CEO or members of the top leadership team, you can be assured that it will be easier to get the attention of all the people below that ranking. Another way to think about who you need to inspire, when it comes to ranking the decision makers, is to consider the following:

- Who is the primary decision-maker?
- Who is the secondary decision-maker?
- Who has the power of veto?
- Who are the key influencers?
- In a world of competing resources, who might want to influence against your idea?

If your preferable is very role-specific, for example if you are the director of sales and your desired future outcome is a creative new digital channel to market, then you may just need to convince your boss and inspire your team to invest time in business development via a new non-traditional route to market. It may also require a business plan for investment in new technologies and new sales enablers. You may find that your creative idea is very welcome and you are praised for your initiative.

However, if your vision is about changing the organization business model entirely, or long-term investments, you will have to go further to galvanize your peers and the top leadership team. Depending on how people rate you, and your ideas, or the costs involved, or the timings versus other company investment priorities, you may meet considerable pushback.

If your preferable is more cause-based for the entire firm – such as achieving equal representation of women in the top 100 leaders of your firm – then your ultimate audience is the CEO and the board. If it difficult to reach them, you could approach a senior female leader to speak to the cause and try to secure support from industry experts, peers and top leaders.

If your vision is more global, such as improving the quality of leadership in the world, then as a first win you may want to secure a mandate to redevelop your company's leadership development programmes. On a bigger scale, you may want to engage with your industry bodies, and even with more national and international organizations like DAVOS and the United Nations.

Even if you currently have no team, no support and no power base to begin with, could you inspire and mobilize peers, customers and any other key stakeholder groups within your access? In other words, no matter how global your vision and no matter how under-resourced you are now, think of where to start and one positive action will lead to another. A 1,000-mile journey starts with a single step! Within your own domain of influence, what can you and your peers do to role model the change you want to see?

Building influence is not a transactional event. It is a journey of a thousand mindful steps. Instead of thinking 'this is what I want, now how do I influence you to give it to me?' you should be continuously building up a reservoir of goodwill with influencers over time, so that when you have an ask, you are already well positioned with the right people. Invest forward by nurturing relationships, show goodwill to people and be consistent in your behaviours. Help as many people as you can along the way.

Building influence is not a transactional event. It is a journey of a thousand mindful steps.

Everything on the list in Table 4.1 is important. However, clarity of purpose and agenda, and values alignment are critical for ambitious future shaping. If you talk about your purpose and agenda, then people can understand what you stand for, and believe in you, and respect you for having a higher mission. If you live your values, people can appreciate your authenticity and feel safe with you because they feel that your behaviour is anchored

TABLE 4.1   What builds influence?

Clarity of purpose and agenda	Know explicitly what you want to achieve, and why; and be able to communicate that to others.
Having a great reputation	Build up a strong reputation for reliability and getting things done through consistency of results and behaviour. You don't want a reputation for being all talk and no action.
Reciprocity	Warm up your important relationships. Before you ask for any support from an influencer, use the principle of reciprocity – ie do a favour for them first. People are hard-wired to want to repay you when you need something from them.
Status	If you are already very well networked and in a position of power or influence, such as being the leader of a team, people are more inclined to agree with you and more willing to do what you say.
Likeability	It is not enough to be likeable but it goes a long way to help. If people like you, they will be more open to your persuasion. At a minimum, they are more likely to listen and hear you out.
Values alignment	When people feel aligned with you on a set of values and principles – and if/when your asks are aligned with what they believe in, you have a way to persuade them to join you. So, before you describe your vision, you could try to get people to commit to a set of values and principles upfront, and let it provide context for support for your preferable.
Social proof	Encourage people via 'social proof' – that because others are doing it, they should also join in.
Scarcity	If you can state or imply that there is urgency or only a short window of opportunity, people are more likely to be persuaded that now is the time to act.

and not unpredictable. The closer your values align with others, the easier it is for them to trust you and support you.

Investment – secure resources to build your team and finance your plans

Everyone loves to hear new ideas and it is always exciting to talk about possible future outcomes. But the real pressure test of whether decision makers are truly inspired or not by your vision is if they will resource it – with their time, their money, their teams and their ideas. To get your ideas off the ground, the right team and the right budget matters more than anything. You could have all the relationship goodwill in the world, but you need a high-quality team of people and actual dollar investment to really make a difference and achieve your desired outcomes.

You will need to convince would-be investors that the future outcome is worthy of the necessary investment and resource allocation. The would-be investor could be your boss or someone outside the organization – whoever has the ability to open their budget purse-strings and finance your plans. Although you and your followership are able to imagine or visualize the future outcomes, the 'accountants' may not fully understand neither the idea nor the return on investment strategy. Some people have to experience something in reality before they truly grasp what you meant.

How large an appetite does your company really have for change? How often do we hear about the desire from the top for more innovation and yet, in cut throat competitive environments, a wrong investment spend may have serious consequences for the future of a business. Even though risk-taking is what will ultimately save companies, there is often a low-risk appetite to spend any money at all on innovation!

To increase your chances of securing sufficient people and monetary investment for your preferables, you will need to adjust your argument from its meaningfulness to why it also makes commercial sense.

How to pitch your business case to budget holders and investors

Articulate your vision in commercial terms: You need to demonstrate your competitive advantage in your chosen idea and explain why your particular approach will succeed. 'Are you solving a real problem? What is your unique advantage?' The analytically minded investor will want to see facts and figures, comparable examples or proof of early concept testing. When it comes to investors, they are less likely to get excited by the dream of what could be, and more excited by well-founded promises of return on investment within specific timelines.

Test your ideas with customers: Where relevant, do some early testing to measure demand for your ideas. Identify the market for your ideas – and sample size it. You don't need to run a professionally quantifiable research process to start with, if you don't have access to funds. You could even just start with a customer quote as reaction. If the customer says something like 'I love it – it could transform our working relationship' or some such gold dust of a quote, then you can take this to your boss or would-be investor. If you share your ideas with customers and they have a very positive strong reaction then this is something you can definitely use to persuade others to invest in you. Document the customer quotes and reactions and share with your internal decision-makers. Gather any relevant data from your customers that support the merit of the proposed idea and future outcome.

Prepare your business plan: A well thought-out and comprehensive business plan is essential to any investment proposition. Include detailed and plausible information on where you see the business and return on investment in three to five years, along with critical success factors. Think through every area of interest that an investor might have when looking at your future shaping proposal, and have all the answers covered when you go in to bat for the budget. Your business plan should show ambition, but growth levels must be achievable, with allowance made for sufficient resource to invest in the business.

Ask for the right people resources: Your pitch should clearly demonstrate the capabilities and competencies of your team, any gaps and the recruitment plan necessary. You need to give assurance to your investor that with the right level of investment in people resources, you and your team have the skills and experience to manage the business idea and will be able to maximize its potential. Don't set yourself up as the hero. Your investors will want to see a shared spread of skills and talent across the team, so that their risk is not over-invested in you as a single person.

Share potential risks and don't embellish the truth: Bosses and investors don't like surprises – they demand honesty and transparency. The quickest way to lose a potential investor is to sacrifice trust by embellishing the truth. Integrity is the name of the game and no business proposal is ever entirely problem free. So don't bury the potential risks, or focus only on the positives – just tell it like it is. Investors can build risk into their decision and into the financials – and while some investors are cautious, others have an appetite for the higher rewards that come with higher potential risk investments.

Suggest a first step – for example a prototype, pilot or customer research: When it comes to options to deliver on the vision, there may be different routes to arriving at the ultimate destination. Present a range of options with pros and cons. Adjust options according to anticipated concerns of investors. Perhaps a prototype or pilot investment should be requested prior to any further big ask. Try to phase in your approach to give it the best possible shot at succeeding in the long term.

SAMPLE BUSINESS PLAN TEMPLATE

1 The problem
Begin with a compelling articulation of the customer problem or opportunity.

2 The solution
Share your idea and how it will address customer pain or add to their delight.

3 Your target market
Describe/attempt to quantify your target market.

4 Your revenue or business model
Be specific about products/pricing and how you plan to make money.

5 Your successes: early traction and milestones
Build credibility. What have you and your team accomplished to date?

6 Customer acquisition: Marketing and sales strategy
Explain how you will reach your customer.

7 Your team
List the strengths and skills on the team, and the extra talent you need to acquire/by when.

8 Your financial projections
What are your 3–5-year projections, backed up with assumptions?

9 Your competition
What is your value proposition versus your competitors'?

10 Your funding needs
How much you need, why you need the money, what it will be used for and the intended outcome.

Try to find the easiest path to the budget you need. It may be useful to identify what budgets are available. For example, within your organization there may be a specific fund for innovation and you may be able to access this if your idea fits the criteria. If your ideas are about responsible business or corporate social responsibility, or the progression of women or minorities, then there is often an existing budget allocation for this type of desired innovation in your organization.

Without proper investment, your vision will not get off the ground. Don't ever underestimate the importance of securing the right funding to ensure you give your vision every chance to succeed. Securing budgets and funding will be an ongoing effort throughout your leadership career – there is always competition for resources.

Finally, don't give up! Talk to any visionary, entrepreneur or intrapreneur and they will share with you what it took for them to convince others. It is not easy, but if you really believe in your vision of the future, it will be worth it. Taking action is very empowering. Do nothing, nothing will happen. Do something, and something might happen! You may get rejected at first – but be resilient. Renew and come back stronger next time. If you believe in your vision of the future, you will have the drive to try again. Remember it's not how many times you get knocked down that count; it's how many times you get back up! The next chapter is all about persistence in the face of obstacles and challenges.

Key takeaways

- Leadership requires followership. Think about your people and key stakeholders and how to inspire and engage them to get involved in supporting you and shaping your preferred future outcome.
- Appreciate that meaningfulness is the new motivation for the millennial generation. Understanding this, communicate your purpose and passion, why the preferable outcome matters to you and why it should matter to them.
- Work out who really matters and what really matters in terms of key influencers and decision makers, in order to secure the wider buy-in and support you will need to achieve your preferable.

- The real pressure test for your ideas is whether the key budget holders will provide you with the team and financial resources required for implementation. Back up your ideas with a business plan setting out your future objective with associated strategies and costings for how to achieve it.

CHAPTER FIVE

Persist: be resilient and stay the course

In an uncertain climate, 'persistence' is arguably the most important competitive weapon left in any leader's toolkit. Business battles are won and lost not on the basis of whether your idea is good or not, but on how persistent you are in sustaining your position and progress. In this chapter I emphasize the importance of being persistent and steadfast in the face of all obstacles. Having agreed on a preferable outcome, and galvanized support and followership, you need the necessary courage of your convictions to stay the course when the going gets tough. This is the secret sauce of successful future shaper leadership.

There are three key aspects to how to be more resilient and stay the course:

- Inner resolve – do you have what it takes to keep going?
- Inhibitors – anticipate what may block your progress.
- Intrepidness – appreciate the role of failure as part of your learning journey.

The implementation phase of your plans is always the hardest of your journey. Let's explore whether you have what it takes to follow through and execute your ideas. The ideation and visioning part of the leadership role is quite exciting. It is fun to talk about great future outcomes, and imagine a better future. It can even be relatively straightforward to get people on side at the beginning, as they feed off your excitement and the possibilities of a better future. Then, in comparison, it is quite 'boring' to have to do the hard work to make it happen. In comparison to the appreciation of what it takes to be a great athlete, in the business world I feel that the persistence part of the leadership journey is never overtly given the full attention or merit, empathy and honour it deserves.

To help with implementation, it is useful to anticipate what may block your progress. For example, blockers may include no self-belief, lack of self-discipline and staying stuck on your original course of action instead of being unwilling to course-correct when necessary. I describe common problems and what you can expect, so that we don't shy away from the challenges, but accept them and have a healthy perspective on how to overcome them.

Finally in this chapter, I address the need to appreciate the role of failure as part of your learning journey. In a volatile, disruptive, innovation-driven business environment, 'failure' needs a reframe as 'inevitable and necessary experience along the way'. It would be better for us in our quest to be future shapers if we reframed failure and persistence not as the hard slog, but instead as a way of building up your leadership muscles for this and for future leadership glories. You grow in confidence as you move out of your comfort zone. When you learn from your mistakes you reap the reward forever. Persistence is not just a work skill fundamental; it is also an invaluable life skill. With all that in mind, let's now explore what it means to build that muscle.

Inner resolve – do you have what it takes to keep going?

Whether you believe you can or not, you're right.

HENRY FORD – FUTURE SHAPER

Persistence is the ability to continue moving forward, looking for solutions and working towards success. This skill is also about the ability to confront challenges and retain your resolve – even when the challenges of leadership become extremely stressful or complicated. Of course, it is easy to persist when things are going relatively well, only a few bumps in the road, and we experience evidence of progress, or the end is in sight. When everything is going great, it is easy to be optimistic and to feel like you can conquer the world. When we feel like we are in control, we are happy to make ambitious plans, and we expect to continue to strive and achieve all our goals. However, there are times when we are reminded that we are not in full control of achieving those plans. What starts out as a great plan with good intentions can suddenly become problematic in the face of real-world changes.

The real test of persistence is how you respond when you suffer major setbacks or even a lack of evidence that you are moving closer toward their goals. In this climate of disruption, uncertainty and innovation, failures will be inevitable. How comfortable are you with the idea of failing, and how emotionally equipped are you to get back on your feet and try, try again?

We may have to adjust, course-correct or start all over again on plans when faced with new competition, industry disruption, company ownership changes, losing key customer accounts or when your boss or key sponsor resigns. There are times in our day, week, month or life when absolutely nothing seems to make sense any more and it feels like pushing water uphill. When this happens, your resilience, your positive attitude and your core confidence is critical to your continued success. When everything

FIGURE 5.1   Three key elements of persistence

appears to be going wrong, all you have left is to decide how to deal with it and how to keep moving forward.

Persistence is about resilience and a great personal attitude – supported by a bedrock of unshakeable core confidence. Resilience is not a characteristic that is bestowed on some individuals and not others. It is an actively learned process. In the context of the continuous macro and micro shocks and disruptions of today's world, you must have already developed a degree of resilience to reach your current position. You need to continue to build even more resilience if you want to be a future shaper. Resilience comes from within – a belief in yourself, your idea and the cooperation of others. When all seems lost, you can keep hope alive by believing in the possible. Your belief and positive attitude can fuel you, and fuel others around you when otherwise everyone would have given up.

Without the right optimistic personal attitude, all progress stalls. Your personal attitude gives velocity to everything you do. It sets you up for success in good times, and it helps you get back on your feet in challenging times. Your vision's vulnerability or success is often dependent on your level of optimism. Your ability to stay the course when the going gets tough is the ultimate

FIGURE 5.2 Believe you will prevail

Believe in yourself	Believe in your idea	Believe in other people
• Be confident that you will solve problems as they arise • Accept that you are not perfect; mistakes will be made but can be recovered • Remind yourself of past accomplishments and current strengths	• Focus on the preferable outcome and remind yourself regularly why it is important • Stay positive even when events are not going your way • Dare to ask for what you need to keep your idea on track • Keep your options open so that you can course-correct if necessary, to get to same end goal	• Some people are very willing to help other people. Who can help you? • Find the right sponsor • Develop your support system of mentors and friends

test of whether you really believe in your vision and desire to achieve your preferable.

When we talk about persistence in the face of challenges, it is not just your idea that is being tested, but more importantly your confidence in yourself and your idea. When you meet opposition and people start to doubt you or question your vision of the future, you may have to dig deep and decide if you have the core confidence in yourself and your vision to carry on.

Your level of core confidence is what will give you the edge as a future shaper leader when it comes to thinking big, being assertive, taking risks and making good decisions. Start by appreciating what you have already achieved. Confidence is the capacity to trust ourselves, others and the world – despite uncertainty and the presence of challenge. It is founded on a set of ideas about the world and our place in it. As a future shaper leader in today's dynamic business environment you need a high degree of self-confidence because you have to set direction in the face of unpredictable outcomes and need to convince others to follow you. If you are truly confident in yourself, it follows that others become

If you are truly confident in yourself, it follows that others become more confident in you.

more confident in you. So it starts with you, and your confidence will grow as you grow in experience. It may not be a linear journey. When we move outside of our comfort zone, our confidence often wobbles; as we succeed, our confidence may grow; as we fail at certain times, our confidence may dip. However, rather than be at the mercy of whether you are succeeding or failing, nurture and expand your core confidence whatever the challenges in front of you and even when you make mistakes. If you learn from your mistakes, you can gain confidence in the knowledge that you will know better next time.

Surface confidence – how outwardly confident you look; how you walk and talk, using good eye contact and self-assured body language. Surface confidence is about how others initially perceive you. It is important because it is how you make your first impression with others. You need to look confident for others to believe that you are confident. You can fake this level of confidence but this on its own will not serve you well in the long term.

Derived confidence – how externalities such as your job, your home, the brands you wear or use give you a greater sense of confidence. It is good to be proud of your achievements and what you can afford, but the concern is what happens if you

FIGURE 5.3 The three layers of confidence

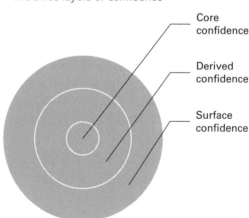

Core confidence

Derived confidence

Surface confidence

suffer a setback in one of the aspects from where you derive your confidence. Your middle layer of confidence can crumble very quickly if you lose your job unexpectedly or you suffer other financial and material losses. Middle-layer confidence is not enough to sustain yourself as a confident leader in today's tough business environment.

Core confidence – an unshakeable sense of self confidence regardless of external events. This is what you need to aim for. As a future shaper leader, you can expect to face a proportionate amount of setbacks and challenges in relation to the ambition of your agenda. It comes with the territory so you need to nurture your core level of confidence and stay robust, resilient and self-reliant when everyone else is looking to you for the answers. This level of confidence is deep, and not easy to develop, but it is good to know what you need to aim for and to pay attention to developing this core layer:

- I feel secure, grounded, calm, determined.
- I trust myself, I trust others, I trust the world.
- I can cope with setbacks.
- I learn from my mistakes.
- I am not easily ruffled or affected by external events.

Future shaper leaders who possess a robust core confidence will more easily overcome fears and uncertainty. Confidence, like all our other emotions, is viral. So by building your core self-confidence, you will transmit this confidence to others and help others to put their confidence in you.

Inhibitors – anticipate what may block your progress

Persistence in leadership is analogous to running a marathon or climbing a mountain. You have a clear outcome in mind, and no matter what happens you are totally focused on getting to the finishing line or the top of the mountain (and in one piece!).

These analogies help, because that's how clear you need to be about your leadership vision. When the going gets tough, it won't be motivating for you to keep going if your vision is blurry, or a series of options, or there is no real definition of what the finishing line will look like. We can all imagine or empathize with the sheer superhuman effort and level of resourcefulness it may require to complete the marathon or climb the mountain. As humans, we get it, we admire it and we cheer from the sidelines when we witness superhumans breaking records or trying something that has never been achieved before – like when the climbers Tommy Caldwell and Kevin Jorgeson captivated the world with their effort to climb the Dawn Wall at Yosemite National Park, a seemingly impossible 3,000-foot rock face. Your journey to achieving your preferable and shaping the future may be just as heroic and similarly as fraught, at times.

A key ingredient to leadership persistence is acknowledging, accepting and anticipating obstacles and challenges.

A key ingredient to leadership persistence is acknowledging, accepting and anticipating obstacles and challenges. It would be naïve to think that all the stars will always smoothly align with your preferred outcomes. This phase of persistence is like the middle piece of the journey – in between setting out your vision and reaching the destination. This is the most vulnerable time for your vision. The middle phase is when your true commitment and effort is under pressure and put to the test.

Let's investigate some classic progress-blockers so that you can get ahead of some common traps and potential pitfalls. To tackle any obstacles and challenges along the leadership journey, here is what you need to consider and sense-check in order to keep going long after most people would have given up:

- #1 Inhibitor – no clear vision/strategic outcome.
- #2 Inhibitor – no driving purpose.

- #3 Inhibitor – no followership.
- #4 Inhibitor – no self-belief.
- #5 Inhibitor – lack of self-discipline.
- #6 Inhibitor – too rigid and stubborn.
- #7 Inhibitor – not politically astute.

#1 Inhibitor – no clear vision/strategic outcome

STOP AND CHECK – DO YOU STILL HAVE CRYSTAL CLARITY
ON THE LONGER-TERM PREFERABLE OUTCOME?

Persistent leaders and teams have a very specific vision in mind that motivates and drives them. Future shapers are visionaries who see their lives as having a higher purpose than simply earning a living. They have communicated this vision to their people and teams, and everyone is inspired to focus on it constantly and with great emotion and energy. Persistence is about building up the confidence of others in the vision – and it is also about eliminating any doubt. After all, you are describing a future state, one that has not yet happened, so the first reaction from others may be doubt, worry or anxiety about the uncertainty of the outcome.

Be ready to communicate and repeat your vision again, and again, and again – especially when people are tired, or suffer setbacks and need re-inspiring. Acknowledge the risks, recognize the uncertainty and be ready to explain why it is still the best idea.

#2 Inhibitor – no driving imperative

STOP AND CHECK – DO YOU REALLY CARE ABOUT THE OUTCOME?

What keeps highly persistent people and teams going is their powerful level of desire. Repeated failures, dead ends, and periods when it seems like no progress is being made often come just before a major breakthrough happens. Persistent people have the inner energy and intensity to keep them motivated and going through these tough times (Deutschendorf, 2015). How much do you really care about the outcome you set out to achieve? Perhaps it is just a theoretical nice-to-have – something to say to impress your boss to land your next promotion. Or do you care enough to stake your personal reputation on the outcome? Are you prepared to take risks, to fail, in the pursuit of figuring out the solution to how to achieve a better future? Are you prepared to have people deride you, are you prepared to ignore any name-calling for daring to want something different and 'impossible'? Without a driving imperative when the going gets tough, you may give in to the pressure and all your efforts collapse. If this does happen, then be honest with yourself about how much effort and resilience it took before you abandoned your position – lots, some or none at all. Now you can take responsibility for any failure to achieve your goals, learn the lesson and move on.

#3 Inhibitor – disengagement/lack of followership

STOP AND CHECK – HAVE YOU BROUGHT PEOPLE WITH YOU
ON THE JOURNEY?

You and your troops have to feel that all the effort will be worth it. This is why meaningfulness is the new motivator. If, at any point, the team starts to feel like they are failing, then a negative spiral kicks in. Feelings of failure or a disconnect from the meaningfulness of the effort leads to lack of motivation, leads to lack of effort, leads to failure and so it goes on in a negative loop. So, how do you keep your teams engaged and motivated during the tough times? Easier said than done, but they have to feel that they are part of a winning team all the time. Keep communicating your vision, keep reminding people of the why, and keep communicating progress. 'Progress' can be a relative term. Perhaps in tough times progress can be reframed as smaller steps, or staying afloat when others are failing, or emotional wins for the team. Morale boosters will be particularly important when the going is tough, so find ways to celebrate or to commune and support each other. Confidence is viral, so as soon as you lose your confidence, it will spread virally across your team of supporters. So, as leader, you need to maintain your confidence levels in the face of all obstacles and challenges. Trust in yourself, and others will trust in you.

#4 Inhibitor – no self-belief

STOP AND CHECK – DO YOU HAVE SUFFICIENT RESERVES
OF CORE CONFIDENCE?

If you don't believe in the vision, or you don't believe in yourself, why would anyone else trust you enough to bat for you? People who overcome the odds and can convince others to follow them have a highly developed sense of who they are and their self-belief can carry on when all else seems lost. Confidence allows the highly persistent to continue on without being greatly affected by what others think of them. While that inner confidence gets challenged and shaken, it never gets destroyed and constantly acts as a source of courage and determination. Do you have sufficient reserves of inner confidence? How do you keep them topped up? What support systems do you have in place to ensure you recover from any confidence setbacks so that you are able to renew your energy and confidence levels for the next day? A simple personal mantra can be very consoling during tough times, such as 'Just keep moving forward' or 'This too shall pass'.

We can take lessons from entrepreneurs on this. With just the germ or seed of an idea, they are able to inspire investors to resource the idea. Even when cash flow is tight, they do what it takes to keep the idea nurtured. All their efforts are forward-focused and nothing will stop them from achieving their vision. They have utter confidence in themselves and their business idea – and are willing to go into personal debt to make it happen. This level of confidence is attractive and an attractor to others – so much that it can become a self-fulfilling prophesy. Confidence breeds confidence. Here is how it goes: I believe so much in this vision, and I have convinced my investors, I have inspired my team, and because of the financial resources and people resources I now have totally stacked the odds in favour of achieving the vision. Confidence breeds confidence.

#5 Inhibitor – lack of self-discipline

STOP AND CHECK - DO YOU HAVE THE SELF-DISCIPLINE
TO KEEP ON GOING?

Highly persistent people know it is very difficult to stay continually motivated, particularly during difficult times and when it appears that no progress is being made. They have come to rely upon their work ethic and self-discipline. They develop habits they can count on to continue down the path towards their eventual goals. They believe the results of the efforts they make today may not be seen for a long time, but they strongly believe that everything they do will count towards their outcome in the end (Deutschendorf, 2015). Do you have the self-discipline to keep going? What about those days/weeks/months when nothing goes right, and it seems more probable that you are heading for an abyss rather than the mountain top? Do you have the self-discipline to keep showing up, to keep trying? Sometimes, showing up is enough to demonstrate to others that you have not given up. In turn, they don't give up – and step by step, you continue to make more progress. Eventually you will turn a corner. Keep your higher vision in mind, and don't give up! More than that, try to enjoy building up your resilience muscles each time you encounter a problem or setback. Eventually you will arrive at a point where nothing can shock you, nothing can break you and you are ready to tackle anything.

#6 Inhibitor – too rigid and stubborn

STOP AND CHECK - ARE YOU READY TO ANTICIPATE
AND COURSE CORRECT?

Please don't confuse persistence with rigid thinking and stubbornness. When self-belief turns egotistic, high achievers start to feel entitled to the outcomes they desire. Face the facts in front of you and be ready to anticipate and course-correct in order to achieve your goals. Don't get stuck in your own way. Persistent people have the ability to adjust and adapt their action plan. They do not stubbornly persist in the face of evidence that their plan is not working, but look for better ways that will increase their chances of success. The highly persistent encounter impasses, and make detours and adjustments until they reach their final destination. They are not tied into their ego and are willing to admit when something is not working. They are quick to adapt the ideas of others that have been shown to work well (Deutschendorf, 2015). It can be quite frustrating when we take a position: it works for a while but then no longer works for us. Have the humility to admit when your approach is not working and you need to seek another course of action. Don't get stuck if you feel you have arrived at a brick wall. Realize when no amount of sledgehammers will break it. Then engage your creative mind, and the minds of those around you to figure out how to course-correct and how quickly. Sometimes it will mean two steps backward in order to go three steps forward – and that's okay too.

#7 Inhibitor – not politically astute

STOP AND CHECK – ARE YOU PROPERLY MANAGING
THE POLITICS OF THE SITUATION?

While it is important to accept that you need to be persistent, don't make life even harder for yourself by not finding smoother paths to your preferable. How can you best align with the politics of your organization so that you can benefit from the slipstreams of current powerful agendas already under way? It is not always possible, of course, but the more politically astute you are, the more you should be able to identify the unifying intersections between your preferable and the preferables of others so that together you can create collaborations and ecosystems to create win–win outcomes. The opposite, frankly, can be a nightmare. If you have to spend all your time on political or petty infighting to achieve what you want, it is very draining and ultimately may threaten your energy levels in being able to persist with achieving your future preferred outcomes. Try to establish cooperative links with other people to gain more support for your ideas – and reduce any blocks. I respect the Taoist saying that says that if you meet an angry horse in an alleyway, then turn back and find another street! Such a nuanced way of knowing when to fight a battle head-on versus finding an alternative 'quieter' and more effective solution is all about being politically astute.

Intrepidness – appreciate the role of failure as part of your learning journey

It is not the critic who counts; not the man who points out how the strong man stumbles, or where the doer of deeds could have done them better. The credit belongs to the man who is actually in the arena, whose face is marred by dust and sweat and blood; who strives valiantly; who errs, who comes short again and again, because there is no effort without error and shortcoming; but who does actually strive to do the deeds; who knows great enthusiasms, the great devotions; who spends himself in a worthy cause; who at the best knows in the end the triumph of high achievement, and who at the worst, if he fails, at least fails while daring greatly, so that his place shall never be with those cold and timid souls who neither know victory nor defeat.

THEODORE ROOSEVELT – FUTURE SHAPER

Embrace every mistake you make as part of your future shaper journey. Own it, learn from it, and take full responsibility for making sure that next time, things will turn out differently. Reframe any failure as the price you have to pay to learn the lesson of your mistake on your future shaper journey. If you learn the lesson, you won't make the same mistake again and this is the dividend that pays out. You will only make the mistake once, but the dividend reaps forever. Don't be afraid to make mistakes; don't be afraid to take risks. Think about risks and mistakes as the route to learning and growing as a future shaper leader. Obviously, we don't seek out failure, but the future shaper leader has to be ambitious, has to think big and take big risks – so, my friends, let's appreciate that failures as well as great successes will be inevitable along the way. See failure as a badge of honour, a rite of passage.

When you let go of any fear of failure, you will feel surprisingly liberated to perform to a higher standard. Instead of worrying about 'what if?' you are freed up to assume it will all work out and to feel confident that even when plans go off course, you will find a solution to get back on track. That way, fear of failure will not hold you back and any actual failure will never devastate you. You will simply put it in perspective and move on. Every successful person has failed along the way – numerous times. In fact, if you follow the logic, then it follows that failure is a crucial part of why they're successful now.

Don't be afraid to make mistakes; don't be afraid to take risks.

As a general observation, I find some cultures, such as the US, are way more open than Europeans about embracing the concept of failure. I remember being told by a student in a London business school entrepreneurship class that when the professor asked the class to raise their hand if they had ever had a business failure, the Americans proudly put their hands up, while the British sat on theirs! The professor, of course, pointed out that the people in the class who had already experienced bankruptcy or business failure were way better positioned for future success than those who were horrified at the very idea of failure and equally horrified at the idea of ever admitting it!

Intrepidness in leadership is about fearless decision making, being the person to take the first step forward and having the ability to meet a challenge or crisis head on. It is important, of course, not to confuse fearlessness with carelessness or recklessness. An intrepid leader is careful, thoughtful and calculates the potential risk before stepping forward to accept a challenge. This is about belief in your abilities and belief in the abilities of the people on your team – your self-confidence creates a sense of confidence in others. Speaking confidently about your team instils confidence in your team and creates high levels of loyalty from your team.

The intrepid leader:

- steps up to the challenge;
- stands their ground;
- is able to go against popular opinion, when necessary;
- rises to the occasion;
- takes the lead;
- is not afraid to raise concerns.

Taken to the maximum, intrepidness could become egoistic as some leaders step up just because they want to cultivate a reputation of leader-as-hero, come to save the day. It is important to be driven by your leadership purpose and imperative when making big risk choices – and balance out any egotistical tendencies by maintaining a strong sense of humility. Always look for ways to share the spotlight.

Do not:

- guess;
- gamble;
- rely only on 'gut instinct';
- be ego-led;
- fall into the leader-as-hero trap;
- take unnecessary risks.

The concept of 'vulnerability' has become a new hot topic in leadership. Traditionally it was seen as a weakness, and a personal liability for leaders. For example, conventional wisdom holds that leadership is only about strength, and that it is difficult to lead or make demands on others from a position of perceived weakness. Traditionally the leader was supposed to know the answer all along, and we all know leaders who are filled with bravado and take great pains to hide any hint of misgivings about themselves or their plans. Recently a more avant garde understanding of vulnerability has emerged, which says that unless you accept your vulnerabilities, you will not be an effective leader. The new thinking promotes vulnerability as an invaluable leadership quality because vulnerable leaders are more authentic and inspire the loyalty of others, which improves bonding and leads to higher performance as a result. Embracing vulnerability means having the emotional courage to address personal fears about the uncertainty of the future. It means a mature understanding of when you might feel ashamed (the fear that you are not good enough) and being emotionally equipped to handle these feelings so that they do not cripple you when the pressure is on. A vulnerable leader decides that they will meet their fears with an open heart, willing to experience all the ups and downs that come with an uncertain future. Vulnerable leaders know they can confront brutal realities head-on while maintaining faith they will ultimately prevail. Once a leader decides to be open and emotionally 'all-in', more positive outcomes follow. When leaders are vulnerable, they are more open and emotionally available, which creates more bonding opportunities and improves team performance.

Future shaper leaders do not have to be perfect in order to be successful. Quite the opposite. Admitting mistakes, being open and honest, and accepting foibles and flaws yields far more effective results than projecting an untouchable facade. Tough leaders may inspire through fear or intimidation. Vulnerable leaders inspire with authenticity and humanity. Authenticity and humility are more likely to sustain better results from people and teams.

STEVE JOBS – FUTURE SHAPER

Sometimes when you innovate, you make mistakes. It is best to admit them quickly, and get on with improving your other innovations.

I'm convinced that about half of what separates successful entrepreneurs from the non-successful ones is pure perseverance.

STEVE JOBS

Steve Jobs was one of the most influential innovators, entrepreneurs and business leaders in history, who changed the world through technology. He alone revolutionized three multi-billion-dollar industries – personal computing, mobile phones and the music industry. More importantly, he transformed the way people read, play, work and live. Steve Jobs' business accomplishments and decisions have greatly impacted our lives, from the smart and attractive outlook of glass-faced smart devices to our access to songs, movies, animation and software developments. A mastermind of technological innovation and corporate vision, Steve Jobs was responsible for making Apple the company it is today.

However, his past was littered with failures, setbacks and crushing defeats. Jobs started Apple in 1976 and the company began to take off, but after an unsuccessful product launch in 1985, Jobs was kicked out of his own company. Most ordinary people would have given up at that point, but instead, Jobs founded a new company called NeXT. NeXT was considered unsuccessful as well, at least for a time, until it caught the eye of a struggling Apple in 1997. Apple purchased the company and brought Jobs back into a leadership position, which he used to develop and launch Apple's breakthrough products, including the iPod, iPhone and iPad. Perseverance is everything. Because he committed himself to doing great things, Jobs was able to work past his personal and professional failures, and eventually leave behind a monumental and unprecedented legacy.

Source: www.brainprick.com

In the end, none of this matters, not even persistence, if you don't eventually achieve the right results – proving your efforts were all worth it. The next future shaper fundamental is 'Prove' and it is about how to nurture successful teams and deliver the right results.

Key takeaways

- Because of the complexity and uncertainty of the business and world environment, you have to find a way to persist and cut through if you want to achieve anything.
- Confidence in yourself and your idea is critical. If you are not confident, how can you expect others to have confidence in you?
- Accept and expect challenges and obstacles along the way to securing the future outcome you desire. Anticipate as much as possible the more obvious potential blockers to your preferable, and take action in advance to mitigate.
- Take calculated risks and embrace failure as the necessary price you pay along the way to learn and grow as a future shaper leader. You do not need to be perfect to be successful. Don't be afraid to be vulnerable. Admit your mistakes; be open to learning from others.

CHAPTER SIX

Prove: nurture successful teams and deliver the right results

There is no point in having clear preferables, persuading others to follow you, persisting against all the odds – and then not achieving great results! The results ultimately justify the effort involved, and give you confidence for more ambitious future-shaping.

There are three key aspects to how you nurture successful teams and deliver the right results:

- Invigorate – rethink your approach to build a winning team.
- Include – foster more resilient teams via diversity and inclusion.
- Impress – achieve early wins and create positive spirals of success.

Critical to the 'prove' component of the future shaper formula is how skilled you are at nurturing a winning team. It starts with a reframe of how to recruit the best people. Rather than the traditional model of recruiting people on seniority and experience, it is time to rethink your approach to build a winning team by opening up the field to candidates based on new criteria of intelligence, growth mindset, resilience, experience, energy and potential. You will also need to create the right environment for your team members to flourish. Your team members are also both exhausted and exhilarated by the opportunities and challenges they face every day. So, how will you empower and equip them to sustain themselves? The future shaper leader will have to establish a new type of environment – more nurturing, more playful and more creative while still setting high standards for a strong work ethic and delivery of good results.

Take charge of your recruitment strategy, with the awareness that resilience and creativity are natural attributes of diverse team members. The term 'diverse' refers to women, ethnic minorities, the LGBTQ community and any other under-represented groups. However, in addition to a targeted recruitment strategy, you also have to pay strong attention to continually removing barriers to an inclusive environment. You will need strategies to surface and address unconscious bias – yours and others' – to ensure that diverse team members are empowered to have an equal voice and that their contribution to the team is optimized.

Finally, you will need to achieve early wins and create positive spirals of success. Your vision may be too large, too daunting and too far away (years or a decade) away from realization – and while you may be comfortable with long-term horizons, they can be counterproductive to your team's morale and motivation. It is smarter to reframe long-term preferables into interim short-term goals with tangible results. The achievement of short-term wins act as a morale booster and allow your team to focus on making steady progress and keep them motivated to stay working towards the larger goal.

Invigorate – rethink your approach to build a winning team

The real winners in business will be those future shaper leaders who know how to build better teams to face the challenges and constant pressures of today's climate; the uncertainties, the disruption, the demand for innovation and the shifting landscape. How do you, as a future shaper, get better at building and leading your teams with this context in mind? Future shaper leaders understand that in today's relentless climate – in the same way they need to rethink their own approach and skills – a radical change of approach is required in how to lead their people and teams.

Whether you are forming or reforming your team to deliver on your future shaper preferables, think less about the 'build' and the architecture of the team – number of people, seniority levels, pay grades. Holding your preferable in mind, shift from a traditional view of what you need from team members and think more about the raw talent ingredients of intelligence, growth mindset, resilience, experience, energy and potential. These are the more critical must-have team member competencies for delivering the results you need, in our shape-shifting environment. It is a skill set that equips team members to cope with uncertainty, to be able to shift gears quickly when necessary, to have the right attitude to cope with constant change. It also liberates you to choose team members without any limits on age or current seniority. Of course, experience is still important, but when you are future shaping, younger people are usually more tapped into the zeitgeist of today and what consumers really want or what the world needs now. Don't create power distances between yourself and those who are digital natives and at the cutting edge of consumerism and futurism.

Recruit future shaper teams on the basis of the right blend of:

- intelligence;
- growth mindset;
- resilience;
- experience;
- energy;
- potential.

TABLE 6.1   Your future shaper team – recruitment criteria

Intelligence	**Bright, smart, clever people** Seek out people for your teams that are fundamentally smart, open and able to learn new skills quickly, willing and capable of processing new information quickly, and have the intellectual capacity to reverse or make new decisions based on new information. Look at their previous successes, and recruit on track record.
Growth mindset	**The opposite of a fixed mindset** In a fixed mindset, people believe their basic qualities, like intelligence or talent, are simply fixed traits. They spend their time documenting their intelligence or talent instead of developing them. They also believe that talent alone creates success – without effort. This is a type of stuck mindset that is self-limiting. In a growth mindset, people believe that their core abilities can be developed through dedication and hard work – and that brains and talent are just the starting point. These people have a love of learning and a progressive attitude that is essential for great accomplishment. You will need team players with a growth mindset – people with the right attitude for an uncertain and unpredictable business world, where it is essential to keep growing and learning and adapting to a constantly changing business environment.
Resilience	**Ability to persevere when the going gets tough** Resilience has probably become the most important currency of the disruption era. It is the capacity to recover quickly from tough challenges and sudden setbacks. Find people who have demonstrated proof of perseverance in life or work, ie examples of having bounced back quickly from any failures and ability to renew their approach if the current one is not working.

(continued)

TABLE 6.1 (Continued)

Experience	Ability to pattern-spot, and a maturity of approach
	Experience brings a maturity and wisdom to the table, which is of huge value when it comes to spotting patterns in advance, not repeating previous mistakes and making suggestions on how to anticipate and mitigate future issues.
	The downside to experience is only when mental fatigue or a general malaise sets in and some people tip into a fixed-mindset, 'we tried that before, and it didn't work' versus the growth mindset of 'let's try again, because the timing and conditions are more conducive now'.
	Recruit people onto your team who bring good judgement from the wisdom of experience, without any negative baggage such as lack of drive to try new things and new ways of working.
Energy	Passion and drive
	Energy is about motivation, passion, commitment and drive. You can be very experienced, but lacking the energy and drive for new challenges. Energy is the velocity and forward momentum necessary to get you to the end state.
	Find people who thrive on challenges, have something to prove, and a relentless drive to succeed.
Potential	Future capacity for development
	Potential is about the latent qualities or abilities that may be developed and lead to future success. In an ever-accelerating pace of change in the marketplace, leaders are recognizing that the most important thing about employees is not where they come from (past achievements), but how far they can go (future potential).
	Find team members who demonstrate their constant willingness and capacity to learn and grow, and have a keen desire to stretch themselves and fulfil their potential.

Depending on your access to talent and resources, not everyone available to you will possess all of the above. However, it sets the standard for what would be an ideal blend for a future shaper team. You can re-enforce your standards through your performance management systems and how incentives and bonuses are awarded. Strive for the ideal. Until then, try to shape the team to be the sum of the parts, and this in itself will support you in creating a competitive advantage. Use the six criteria to create a standard and expectations when briefing your HR and recruitment partners. Communicate your standards regularly to set the bar high with your team members about what is important for this team to be successful.

Whenever possible, hire people better than you. Be fearless about this.

Whenever possible, hire people better than you. Be fearless about this. It will raise your game, it also means that you are serving the greater good, and not just protecting your ego as leader. Your role becomes about maximizing the talent on your team, and developing opportunities for your people to fulfil their potential. You will gain a reputation for hiring the best, and giving your people the opportunity to shine – as a result, the best people will flock to join your team and you will increase your chance of achieving your preferable.

Even when you don't have a role vacancy, always stay on the lookout for fresh talent. Be attentive to the talented people around you and be constantly vigilant of who you could recruit on to your team; scanning your team, other people's teams, industry network conferences and events. Have an expansive attitude and know that there is always room for more talent on your team. Always be on the alert for talent internally and externally. And, of course, make sure there is as much focus on nurturing and developing your team as there is on recruiting new people on to it.

With the right blend of talented people on board, your ongoing task is to establish a nurturing team environment that empowers your people to bring their best to the table. Inspired by the best of what I have observed in so-called 'millennial-friendly' work environments, I stepped back to reflect on a successful environmental model for future shaper team success. I recommend a deliberately constructed and curated environment to offer people with experiences and opportunities to work, play, create, share, learn and grow. These are not entirely separate activiites but are instead seamlessly blended into the daily experience. To avoid burnout at one end of the spectrum, and to create the conditions for team members to be inspired and to innovate, we need to continuously calibrate the right environment to lead and nurture our teams.

Work – the kind of work you need to offer the type of bright and talented team members I describe needs to be meaningful, stretching and connected to a higher purpose. Without a clear line of sight to an important preferable outcome, roles can

FIGURE 6.1   Nurture your team

become demoralizing for bright and talented people. Future shaper team members will want to feel that their work matters, that their investment of time and energy matters. The future shaper leader will need to inspire their team with their vision of the future, their vision of what is possible and galvanize their team to follow them, to contribute, to help shape and deliver the preferable outcome. This will involve including team members in future shaping, in decision making, in developing ideas on what will work. It means providing opportunities and giving responsibility. It means empowering team members to course-correct when strategies are not working, and trusting team members to find new ways of arriving at the preferred destination.

Play – play is about creating pressure-valve release for your team members. Silicon Valley organizations have taken this to the max with in-office arcade games, replacing stairs with fun slides and chutes, on-site gyms, free cooking classes, and sleeping pods for those who need a rest from work and play. Sports and social events are a big part of the 'university campus' feel of social technology companies. Without infantilizing your people, think about what you can do to create time and physical space for play for your team – to support the alleviation of their work pressures and to nurture their ability to de-stress and renew their energy for the next task ahead.

Create – empower your people to be innovative and to create solutions for the challenges they face. In other words, agree on what needs to be done but don't micro manage on the how. Let that be up to the individual. Try to remove limits as much as possible. Give people freedom to be creative – and see what they come up with. You must always hold people accountable for the outcomes agreed, and by when – but encourage and trust your people to find new ways of working. Support your people to be digitally enabled, and as much as you can, release people from the shackles of any corporate bureacracy.

Share – keep lines of communication open, with each other and across the team. Establish the shared team mission, assign roles and responsibilities, and ensure that team-playing is a critical component of the success of the team. Expect team conflicts – too many or none at all are equal red flags and you may require expert help from outside the team if you cannot resolve any extreme issues. Set high standards on how you expect the team to behave with each other – for example 'respect for each other' – and back this up by role modelling good behaviours.

Learn – stimulate learning and cross-fertilization of ideas across the team through regular debate and discussion. Stay open to all suggestions, especially welcome when anyone challenges the status quo. Invest in learning platforms and strategies to support reskilling and digitial enablement. Balance your investment in learning development dollars on emotional intelligence as well as artificial intelligence. Emotional intelligence is the capacity to be aware of, control and express one's emotions, and to handle interpersonal relationships judiciously and empathetically. For now, humans still have the edge over the robots on relating, caring and creativity. Whatever the future of robots, let's continue to improve our humanity and social connectedness with each other, so that trust grows, loyalty grows, social bonds grow and we build better teams as a result.

Grow – provide your people with stretch opportunities to grow. Empower and equip people with innovative technologies, making workers what Accenture calls 'human+', ie each person brings a constantly growing set of technological capabilities to the job alongside their own individual knowledge, experience and skill set. Becoming human+ has expanded the capabilities of the workforce beyond what companies could have imagined just a few decades ago. It is one of the biggest wins from the era of digital transformation. Organizations can draw on a workforce with a constantly evolving set of capabilities to achieve innovation on a grand scale (Daugherty, Carrel-Billiard and Biltz, 2019).

Include – foster more resilient teams via diversity and inclusion

Diversity within your team is not only an equality imperative but is a critical strategy for business and leadership success in these challenging times. You need to find strategies to unleash the potential of your people to drive or respond to disruption and exploit the potential of the Fourth Industrial Revolution. One very interesting way to activate a more creative and resilient team is to recruit more people from diverse and minority backgrounds. It is better understood now that team members from diverse backgrounds expand innovation and strengthen customer relationships, and are also more resilient as a natural result of what they have to endure in order to survive and thrive in a system that is institutionally biased against them. They have to endure more than the average person just to be in the room. Over time this endurance has become an embedded core strength in the face of obstacles and change. Studies show that diversity also increases resilience across the team; like biological communities, companies that encompass more heterogeneity are better positioned to withstand unanticipated changes. There is a positive influence and spread of resilience through good role-modelling and the introduction of new behaviours and approaches into the team culture and environment. This represents such a fantastic opportunity for the future shaper leader to leverage diversity for competitive advantage.

Diversity increases the capacity for innovation by expanding the range of a company's ideas and options. The most obvious sources of diversity, such as gender, ethnicity and sexual orientation, are indeed important in driving innovation. But a variety of work experience and educational background are also meaningful – and teams that are diverse on multiple dimensions are even more innovative. To unlock the full potential of diversity, the future shaper leader needs to foster a team culture conducive to embracing new ideas; they must install enabling measures like open communication practices and a commitment to building diversity into the business and team strategy.

Diversity is a reality. Inclusion is a choice. Although we have made huge strides in technology and sophisticated business offerings, it is confounding that we are still grappling with the basics of how to include more women in senior management teams and at the top leadership table. It is unacceptable that leadership teams continue consciously or unconsciously to exclude female membership. It's not just about women – organization leadership teams do not adequately reflect the multicultural and diverse society we all live in. Systemic issues and unconscious bias are at play in society and in organizations and there are no quick fixes. As such, future shapers need to be very mindful about bias and exert more conscious effort into examining the role they play in recruitment and development, and on being more proactive in promoting inclusion and diversity. More creative recruitment strategies will be necessary to tap into talent sources that can bring fresh ideas and find and explore new markets and new customers.

If you work in a big corporate, you may be familiar with 'diversity and inclusion (D&I)' as a term, and no doubt there may be a D&I initiative under way in your firm. Typically, it manifests as activities to increase the proportion of women in senior leadership roles. It may involve courses for management on 'How to reduce unconscious bias' and placing more emphasis on skills and potential during recruitment and promotion rounds – versus choosing in the same image. Regardless of the enthusiasm for initiatives, there seems to be slow progress on real change. For example, some women are still not paid equally even when represented within senior levels of business. There are many other minority groups such as ethnic groups, or members of the

Diversity is a reality. Inclusion is a choice.

LGBTQ community and more who feel that they do not have enough leadership role models. Rather than seeing diversity and inclusion as an initiative, future shaper leaders understand that inclusion needs to be embedded in the business strategy and is not a 'special project' or a nice-to-have.

Awareness of conscious bias on its own is not enough. Future shaper leaders will need to instil conscious inclusion in their leadership strategy and team culture. Inclusion is about an ability to break down barriers and integrate diverse individuals and groups, as well as being open to diverse thinking and unconventional approaches. Inclusive leadership is about having a progressive mindset backed up with a real action plan:

- Diversity and inclusion embedded within your core strategy, and not a separate HR people management initiative.
- Remove any obsession with 'fit' as part of your recruitment strategy. If you or your recruitment representatives continue to search for people who 'fit' with the company culture, then real inclusion will never be realized.
- Be alert to and remove barriers – real or perceived – in order to create a working environment where each person feels confident that they will have their views heard and represented.
- Be a role model for inclusion, be open to challenge when you are displaying your own unconscious bias. Work with the team on the how.
- It is not enough to talk about being more inclusive. Pay conscious attention to surfacing and removing unconscious bias within the team. It takes time and effort but the business advantage is worth it.
- Respect and appreciate the unique value of the individual as well as the group. Embed the mantra that the best from everybody equals the best for everybody.
- Appreciate that people perform better when they can be themselves and bring their best selves to work.

Impress – achieve early wins and create positive spirals of success

Consider what could be your early wins. What impact you could make, that delivers on a tangible quick win – showcasing to stakeholders your ability to deliver value early, as an indicator of future success. This can range from a physical prototype, to a highly impactful change of processes, to a new customer win. Don't expect stakeholders to wait for the big payout at the end – show some goodwill and good value early on. It buys you time, as you consolidate your efforts for delivering on the bigger picture. The faster you establish a pattern of impressive results, the easier it will be to secure further backing for your current and next future shaper ideas. The psychology of winning is very important to your stakeholders and your team – people feel more motivated to perform if they feel that they are achieving their goals. If the team feels like it is failing, with all the odds stacked against them, it is very hard to turn up every day and continue to give 100 per cent. However, when the team feels like it is making a difference, that what they do is contributing to something important, and results are in sight and just keep coming, then they will give extra and be extra satisfied when the wins come. *Winning creates a very positive spiral effect; success follows success.* Talented people are more likely to want to join your team if it has a reputation for positive results – and having more talented people on your team will lead to more wins. Your journey to shaping the future becomes smoother with every win banked.

Great results will come from a clear understanding of the preferable outcome, and an alignment of the right people in the right roles, all motivated to achieve that mission. You need to communicate your end goal and your interim goals in a way that is crystal clear to the team, and which inspires them and motivates them to help you achieve. However, as discussed in Chapter Four on 'persuade', you can't assume that everyone will immediately buy in to your vision. Rather than 'tell' your vision, try to bring people on the journey of the 'why' it is important and enlist their support. Stay with the bigger picture when first describing the vision, the why and the preferable outcomes your team needs to achieve, and by when. The team mission is about how the team will achieve the preferables. Break down the preferable outcomes into steps or phases, if that is useful. For example, state the preferable outcomes to be achieved within three years, the first 12 months' priorities and what therefore needs to be done in the next 100 days.

Being an effective communicator means that the communication has to be two-way. You need to be a good listener as well. The team will have knowledge and opinions of their own, which could help enhance your own understanding of the current state of play, and what could be achieved and by when. Share perspectives, discuss options and agree together on a plan and path forward.

Ultimately, your leadership success will be judged against the achievement of great results by you and your team. It is very important that you know how to build a successful team and that they deliver on time and on budget, again and again. Consistency is very important for your future shaper leadership reputation over the long term. In cases where the mission is extremely challenging to fulfill or targets will be missed, then it becomes critical to know how to manage the expectations of key stakeholders. The only outcome worse for a future shaper leader than missing targets is when it is an unexpected shock to your boss or stakeholders. It makes you look out of control and unreliable. The trick is to gain a reputation for being consistent at hitting your targets, or finding any issues early on and managing expectations accordingly. If you are known as someone who can be reliable in good times and bad, then it will be easier for people to trust you with more responsibility even when the stakes are high. It is not always possible to reliably deliver if you are involved in high-risk manoeuvres to bring a new product to market or transform the organization; however, your messaging can incorporate reliability even in the most turbulent of times. For example, 'I will always tell the truth', 'I have a no-surprises policy' and 'I operate with full transparency'.

Create early foundations for team success: what not to do

In order to create successful outcomes, it might be worth looking at what not to do. There are some common mistakes that leaders make with their teams, which immediately get in the way of their success. It is worth noting the list of blockers here so that you are very clear on what not to do:

- no clear team mission;
- not putting the right people in the right roles;
- underperformers remain in role;
- too many 'priorities';
- inadequate resourcing;
- lack of trust;
- fear of conflict;
- lack of commitment;
- silo-thinking;
- no accountability;
- group think;
- team member burnout.

Assembling and nurturing the right team for your future shaping preferable propels its chances of success. However, there is one final component left to discuss before you are fully equipped to make a real impact. In the next chapter, I explain the importance of having a platform – access and reach to the influencers who can give leverage to your efforts. I discuss power and politics,

TABLE 6.2   Developing your future shaper team – what not to do

No clear team mission	When the team mission is not crystal clear, there is no shared effort. You only have a group of individuals working for you and not a 'team'. People start pulling in different directions, and time and energy are wasted. Is your team clear on the big-picture vision and their current shared mission within that context? Does your team collaborate effectively to fulfill the mission?
Not putting the right people in the right roles	It may sound obvious but you need the right people in the right roles suited to their abilities and potential. Your success with teams is the ability to recruit and nurture great talent aligned with the mission of the team, refreshing the talent when the team mission changes, and always inspiring the team to perform to the best of their individual and collective ability. Do you have the right people in the right roles? Are you playing to individual and collective strengths?
Underperformers remain in roles	Issues with unmotivated or incompetent people need to be addressed quickly; be prepared to move people out of the team. By not dealing with underperformers you erode your own standards and risk demotivating your best performers. Team members will be confused if you enable sub-par performers to stay on the team. Are you prepared to act fast when dealing with underperformers?
Too many 'priorities'	Are your team members crystal clear on the priorities of their roles or do you keep adding to their list? Often team members are overwhelmed with too many priorities. If everything is a priority, then nothing is a priority. When you are clear on your preferable outcomes, it will be easier to set or reset priorities in service of the longer-term goals. Do you set clear priorities?

(continued)

TABLE 6.2 (Continued)

Improperly resourced teams	To fulfill your plans, you need the right people in the right roles. Your people also need to be adequately digitally enabled and resourced with the right tools and applications to optimize performance. Do you enable your team to fulfill their roles, and do you equip them to take advantage of digital innovations?
Lack of trust	When people don't trust each other, there is less collaboration and decisions are second-guessed and take longer. Trust usually breaks down when leadership communications break down. Make sure you keep everyone up to speed on your strategic agenda and the reasons why any course corrections are taking place. Are you continuing to regularly communicate your vision and intent? Are decisions made fast enough? Do you trust your team, do they trust you?
Fear of conflict	Sometimes the leader signals to team members that they don't want to hear bad news and they don't want to be challenged on decisions. This is not a helpful culture to create because it shuts down ideas and debate, and better solutions to problems. Are people encouraged to bring a diversity of opinion and to challenge you and each other on how things are done? What can you do to encourage more healthy debate?
Lack of commitment	People may be showing up, but do they really care about the leadership agenda and team mission? Complainers and people with a negative attitude can really drain the energy of those around them. You need committed, passionate people on your team who will go the extra mile and believe in the long-term goals. Is there a sense of can-do and optimism on the team?

(*continued*)

TABLE 6.2 (Continued)

Silo thinking	When team members with a silo responsibility turn up at a team leadership meeting, they need to put their silo hat to one side and add value to the shared needs of the team. Team in-fighting over siloed agendas means that they do not understand the overall mission and why everyone needs to work in service of the higher goals.
	Do you constantly remind people how their silo role fits into the bigger picture, and the value of everyone working together to achieve the vision?
No accountability	Unfortunately, some people are all talk and no action. Unless you are alert to holding people accountable, it can take longer than you think to work this out – especially if the same people are very verbally agile and it sounds as if they are doing their best, but somehow things or people keep getting in the way. Hold people accountable via their actions and deeds, not their words. Check for hard deliverables, and agree interim deliverables along the way.
	Do team members deliver what they say they will deliver, when they said they would deliver it? Are you holding team members to account for their actions?
Group think	Group think occurs when you have an overly cohesive team and not enough exploring of alternative. You should ensure you have at least one challenger or provocateur in the team – whether that is you, or another team member. Surface the concept of group think so that the team are more conscious of the phenomenon and can call it out when they see it happening – aware that it may get in the way of their decision making and creating better solutions.
	Is your team too complacent? Does your team suffer from too much consensus and not enough debate of alternative approaches?

(continued)

TABLE 6.2 (Continued)

Team member burnout	Having to be on 24-7 can lead to team member fatigue and eventual burnout of your best people. You will have to be vigilant about the energy levels of the team, and establish the necessary mechanisms to avoid individual and team burnout. It is all too tempting to just keep driving your team hard, but there needs to be time out after major deadlines for some rest and recovery. Empower your team to take responsibility for their health and energy levels – and be open to their suggestions for better work–life balance. Look for signs that you may be overworking your most conscientious people. Watch out for people who regularly stay too late, with only the cleaner as company. Take notice if you regularly have people on your team who call in unwell.

and how the merit of your idea will not be enough. It is also your ability to play the political game that counts.

MELINDA GATES – FUTURE SHAPER

The world is full of what seem like intractable problems. Often we let that paralyze us. Instead, let it spur you to action.

MELINDA GATES

Melinda Ann Gates is an American philanthropist and a former general manager at Microsoft. In 2000, she co-founded the Bill & Melinda Gates Foundation, the world's largest private charitable organization, with her husband Bill Gates. Despite being the wife of one of the world's wealthiest individuals, Mrs Gates is not always living the cushy life. In fact, she often finds herself in some of the most desperate places on the planet. As co-chair of the foundation, Melinda Gates has been on a future shaping mission to find solutions for people with the most urgent needs, wherever they live.

The foundation has been involved in developing prevention vaccines and treatments for illnesses like malaria, tuberculosis and HIV/AIDS. The Bill & Melinda Gates Foundation has approximately 1,500 employees and total grant payments since inception (through Q4 2018) of $50.1 billion. Along with Bill, Melinda shapes and approves the foundation's strategies, reviews results and sets the overall direction of the organization. Together, they meet with grantees and partners to further the foundation's goal of improving equity in the United States and around the world. Through her work at the foundation over the last 15 years, Melinda has seen first-hand that empowering women and girls can bring transformational improvements in the health and prosperity of families, communities and societies. In 2012, Melinda spearheaded the London Summit on Family Planning, which adopted the goal of delivering contraceptives to an additional 120 million women in developing countries by 2020. Melinda donated a staggering $560 million in 2012 to improve access and availability of contraceptive products to women of third-world nations. Her work has led her to increasingly focus on gender equity as a path to meaningful change.

Sources: www.gatesfoundation.org/who-we-are/general-information/ leadership/executive-leadership-team/melinda-gates; https://live.worldbank. org/experts/melinda-gates; https://richtopia.com/women-leaders/melinda-gates-biography-philanthropy-leadership; https://en.wikipedia.org/wiki/ Melinda_Gates

Key takeaways

- Re-orient your team and talent strategy to the new skills and criteria required now, such as growth mindset, energy and resilience. Establish a nurturing environment to promote more effective team performance and success.

- Embed inclusion into your recruitment and team strategy to build a more naturally resilient and creative team, and leverage diversity for competitive advantage.
- In any new leadership endeavour, bank early tangible wins; and create positive success spirals where one success leads to another and people feel motivated by being part of a winning team. Avoid common team leadership mistakes and remove any barriers to high performance from your people and teams.

CHAPTER SEVEN

Platform: power up your network and multiply your impact

The final critical fundamental of the future shaper leadership intelligence framework is 'platform'. Your platform is your stage, your capacity for accessing and reaching other people. If you have an ambitious future shaping idea, do you have a platform to share it with other people? How many people will pay attention? If you put a priority item on your agenda, does it immediately become a priority item for a large number of other people? Imagine if you had this level of influence – how much easier it would be to achieve your goals, how much easier it would be to shape the future you desire.

There are three key aspects to platform and how to power up your network and multiply your impact:

- Increase – grow your platform to maximize return on effort.
- Intensify – expand your personal power and enhance your reputation.
- Impact – merit alone is not sufficient; ignore politics at your peril.

Think of 'platform' as the secret sauce on how to make maximum leadership impact and sustain your career as a successful future shaper. When you add 'platform' into your recipe, you are giving your ideas a much bigger and better shot at becoming reality. The size of your platform can make an exponential difference to your leadership impact and maximize the return on all your leadership efforts. For example, when a CEO decides to put a future outcome on her agenda, as soon as she communicates it, the whole company hears about it and will act upon it – and all necessary budgets and people resources will be reassigned accordingly to bringing this future outcome into reality. The CEO has a considerable platform advantage on converting preferables into predictables. In lieu of you not having reached that top leadership or CEO platform yet, I offer you a range of suggestions for how you could grow your own platform now.

I also offer you strategies on how to expand your personal power and enhance your reputation, in advance of having the kind of positional power that eventually brings with it more authority and influence. You don't have to wait until you get promoted; you can empower yourself now to have your voice heard.

Finally, this chapter examines the crucial role that corporate politics can play in either providing you with a supportive platform and smoother pathways to your future shaper dreams, or how politics can crush what you set out to achieve. If you ignore the politics around you, in a world of competing resources and competing agendas, then you ignore them at your peril. When the stakes are high, and some key decisions hang in the balance, the currency of politics can make the difference between success and failure in achieving your preferable outcome.

Increase – grow your platform to maximize return on effort

Your platform is the stage that gives you and your future shaping message a chance to be heard by other people. Platform is about reach, voice and visibility – providing you with access and leverage to secure the support of others and help make your future desired outcomes a reality. You need to find ways to make your voice heard so that you gather followership and garner support for your ideas from the people who can help you to bring them into reality. When you have a solid platform of followership and power, you have more authority to continue to influence others and shape the future you desire. The bigger the platform, the bigger your leadership impact. The bigger your platform of contacts and followers, the easier it is for you to shape the future. Without a platform, your great ideas get neither a voice nor visibility and will fall short of what could have been achieved. You could have had the best idea in the world, the most meaningful world-changing legacy idea – but if no one wants to hear it, or act on it, then your vision dies before it really has a chance to get off the ground. If people heard about your vision, but didn't find you credible enough to want to fund your ideas because of your low platform and power base, this too is fatal for your vision. Without any followership or senior platform (yet), it will be more challenging to access resources and support to get your future shaper ideas off the ground.

One obvious direct route to building a strong platform is to continue to get promoted into senior roles as your career progresses. But you don't need to wait for your next promotion to think about platform. There are other strategies regarding what you can do today to amplify your status and grow more followership. Whatever your current level, don't despair – almost every great entrepreneur and intrapreneur and future shaper leader started out just with their vision, and just the seed of an idea; step by step they built their team and business, endured all the setbacks and detours, and grew their business and their platform to the point where their views on how to shape the world are now actively sought out by their team, followers, the public, media and government.

Fortunately, it doesn't have to take years and years to make an impact. What is so very exciting about the business world today is that it is more open and more democratic. Senior executives are more willing to listen to their customers and staff, and there is an appetite from the top to hear good ideas. Organization structures are flatter, new technologies and social media offer tremendous opportunity to young people to grow followers and gain direct access to people in power.

We can start out without any platform whatsoever, and grow it along the way. Think of your capacity to grow your future shaper platform as being similar to how you can grow followership on your Twitter or Instagram account. These social media platforms are open to everyone, so you can access them; in theory you have world influence at your fingertips. Then you just need to figure out how to get people's attention. Similarly, the idea of 'leadership' is like an open platform, and anyone at any level can take up a cause and lead. You can start from a low base of power, and the more you can grow your followership the quicker and easier it will be to make an impact and achieve the future outcomes you want to manifest. The more followers you gain online and in real life, the quicker and easier it is to share your ideas and messages and the quicker and easier it is to make an impact.

We can start out without any platform whatsoever, and grow it along the way.

Conduct a quick stocktake of how many followers you have right now. Think about your peers, team, organization, and family and friends network. In social media terms, consider how many actual followers you have on Twitter, LinkedIn or other relevant social platforms for business. As leader of a team, you have a platform right there. As a leader within your firm, you have a company brand platform. As you continue to secure promotions, you build your positional platform:

- How many followers do you currently have?
- How do you currently share your ideas, and get people's attention?
- Do you belong to a company that offers you a good brand platform?
- Do you have any 'power' relationships to offer you enhanced reach and access to others? That is, relationships with people in strong positions of power who would advocate for you and help smooth the path for resourcing and delivery of your ideas.

Depending on the answers above, how to increase your followership becomes an important question. Platform is not just about your number of followers – it is also about the quality of your followers, and the quality of the relationship you have with them. You don't need to have the support of everyone. Don't get confused by the allure of growing your followership as if it is just a popularity contest. Growing your platform is an ongoing journey of strengthening the relationships you have, and adding more followers. You need to find ways to continue to build your credibility and relationships over time. So that, when you have bigger and bigger ideas to share, you are well positioned with a strong track record over a number of years and a good reputation for delivering results, and people will be more likely to listen to you and take you more seriously.

Apply the following levers to build up your platform:

1 Raise your profile.
2 Gain access to power.
3 Strengthen your relationships.

Each one of these can be further deconstructed, as follows:

1 Raise your profile:
   - Work on high-visibility projects.
   - Speak up at meetings.
   - Participate in strategic cross-functional initiatives.

FIGURE 7.1   Grow your platform

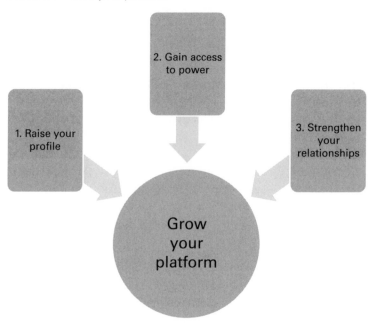

- Stand out from the crowd/don't conform.
- Communicate your accomplishments.
- Become an expert/thought leader on your topic of interest.
2 Gain access to power:
  - Grow your network.
  - Choose the right boss.
  - Find good mentors.
  - Attend key conferences/events.
  - Get promoted to more senior levels.
3 Strengthen your relationships:
  - Impress your boss, customers and stakeholders.
  - Deliver consistently and reliably.
  - Always seek to add value.
  - Help others first, before asking for help.

FIGURE 7.2   Raise your profile

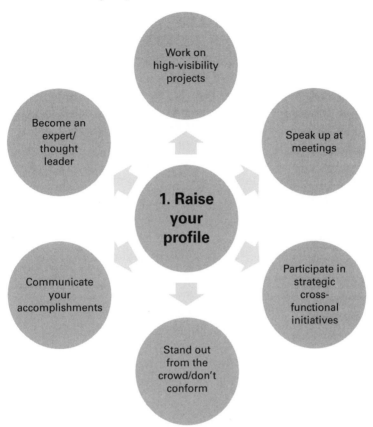

Work on high-visibility projects: if you keep your head down in your own small team or division, no one in the rest of the organization will notice you. Volunteer or ask your boss to put you on high-visibility projects. Usually these are strategy or innovation projects, or major change agenda projects – and you can meet more people and gain more access to senior leadership in your organization.

Speak up at meetings: if you have something interesting to say, say it. When I was a junior, I was a bit apprehensive at first to speak up at meetings, until I realized that I did have valid observations. Sometimes I thought my point was too obvious and surely had already been considered – and then I realized that what was obvious to me was not necessarily obvious to everyone else and that my views were worth sharing. Senior people and clients liked the frankness of my views and noticed me, and were subsequently more likely to pay attention to what I said the next time too.

Participate in strategic cross-functional initiatives: you will learn so much from getting out of your functional area and meeting people from across the firm. It is an opportunity to expand your relationships with people who can access different levers in the organization – for example HR, legal, finance and others. By finding out how other functions work, and developing relationships with people in these functions, you are widening your range of contacts and access to resources.

Stand out from the crowd/don't conform: when everybody is simply nodding their head and going along with what they are being told to do, be unafraid to challenge and question the status quo. Don't be afraid to have your own opinions and not conform, or not follow the crowd. One way of raising your profile is to have an alternative point of view, or a provocation that nobody else has thought of.

Communicate your accomplishments: unfortunately, there are no prizes for being shy and modest about your achievements. Have the confidence to share your achievements and success with others, so that they learn to value and appreciate you and your ideas. The corporate world is especially competitive, and you need to be able to stand up for yourself and communicate your accomplishments, or you may go unnoticed while other noisy but less substantive people take up all the available oxygen and attention.

Become a thought leader: positioning yourself as a market expert and thinker in your particular niche or specialism is a very positive way to raise your profile in your company and industry. Actively managing a reputation in your industry and online for contributing to debates and helping to define the issues and opportunities in your market will raise your profile and boost your reputation no end.

Following on from raising your profile to grow your platform is finding strategies to gain access to power.

Grow your network: I like the analogy of thinking about a bonfire when you think about building your network. Instead of lighting a large number of small disparate fires on

FIGURE 7.3   Gain access to power

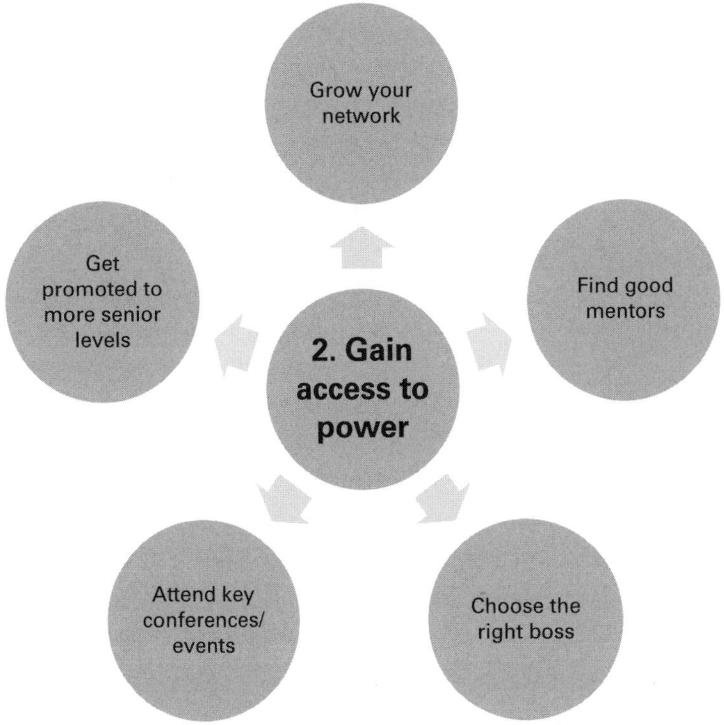

a wide range of topics, choose your central position and build a bonfire instead – stoking it up regularly with new contacts, new value, new sparks. In other words, decide your preferable outcome, and where to invest your time and energy to build a critical mass of relationships that help you to achieve your goal.

EFFECTIVE NETWORKING

Going to networking events, having great conversations and then no subsequent follow up is not the way to build your network. You have to try to turn those conversations into a business relationship by adding value to the other person. You add value to them first, and they will be more inclined to bring you value later on. That may sound quite calculating – and yes, it is! The best relationships are born from mutual benefit, and that goes double for professionals who are building new networks from scratch.

Some people are natural connectors – they know a lot of people, find it easy to make friends and form relationships with the right people who can help spread their message. Great, if that's you! Appreciate your talent in this area and leverage it. If that is not you, then you need to befriend the natural connectors and try to develop your own more targeted networking strategy:

1 Be friendly with everyone, but focus on cultivating a few high-quality connections.

2 Consider who you want to connect with, and why.

3 Become friends with a natural connector who will make introductions for you.

4 Think about how you can help the other person, before asking for anything.

5 Ask for what you want when you have earned the right to ask.

6 Pay it forward; help other people who need your help.

Find good mentors: if you take the initiative to find and cultivate good mentor relationships, you are both gaining from the advice that they can give you and benefiting from the influence, platform and relationships that they have spent years cultivating. Even if there is no official pairing up or mentoring system in your workplace, empower yourself to ask a senior leader to mentor you. Even a business breakfast once a quarter can reap tremendous benefit for you.

Choose the right boss: pick a boss who will give you visibility with more senior people in your organization. There are always strategic initiatives under way in an organization that align with the CEO and top leadership agenda – and require good team members. Could your boss raise your visibility and offer you great experience by assigning you to one of these initiatives? Are they the type of person that will be generous about giving you access to their boss, and other senior leaders in the organization? Find a boss who really cares about your career progression. The right boss is also most likely to be moving quite quickly up the ranks, and perhaps they will take you with them as they rise, which helps you to grow your platform as you become more senior in the organization.

Attend key conferences/events: there is usually a key annual conference in your industry or domain of expertise that is worth attending. Chief Executives like to attend the annual World Economic Forum (WEF) at Davos in Switzerland. You could find out about the opportunities to join the WEF Young Global Leaders group via your organization.

Get promoted to more senior levels: the more you get promoted, the more senior you become, the more automatic access you will have to bigger teams, better budgets and a wider stakeholder audience.

Impress your boss, customers and stakeholders: you need to impress the people you work with if you stand any chance of gaining their support for your more ambitious ideas. Your track record and strength of relationships with your immediate

FIGURE 7.4   Strengthen your relationships

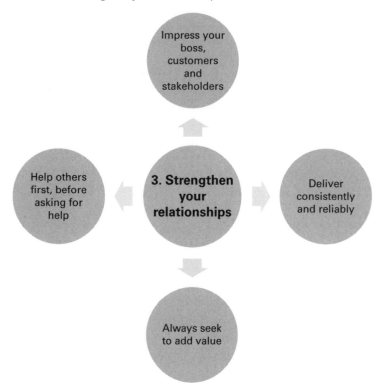

business circle forms the central core of your reputational success. Don't ever take these relationships for granted – continue to nurture and appreciate the people around you.

Deliver consistently and reliably: all your stakeholder relationships will strengthen if you gain a reputation for being consistent and reliable. People will trust you and have faith that you will deliver what you say you will deliver. They will take your ideas and plans more seriously.

Always seek to add value: don't be noisy for the sake of wanting to be heard. Instead, speak up only when you have something value-adding to say, or say nothing at all. This applies to meetings and social media. You don't want to build a reputation for just being noisy on social media, because your important message may be jeopardized by getting lost in the mix of low-value 'entertainment' messaging. Manage your reputation in real life and online.

Help others first, before asking for help: when you help other people first, without obliging them to return the favour, the psychologists say the recipients of your favours will still feel an unconscious obligation to help you back. This builds up a 'favour bank' with other people, which will naturally flow back to you, or that you can hope to draw on as specific needs arise in the future. Of course, some people are all take and no give, so it doesn't work in every case. Try to be natural and don't use reciprocity in too calculated a fashion or people will see through your motives and feel used. This will have the opposite effect and people will resent you helping them.

Intensify – expand your personal power and enhance your reputation

Think about the positional power of presidents and CEOs – the kind of platform they have to make an impact is enormous. Imagine if you are the CEO of a billion-dollar enterprise, with access and reach to half a million employees – that is quite a lot of resource and leverage available to help you shape your future outcomes. Top leaders and CEOs and are very well placed to be future shapers. If you were at that level, you would have reached a position of power and influence and have a willing and 'captive' followership – eager and ready to listen to your ideas, and to act upon them. Aligned with what is right for the company, you would have a window of power and proliferation; where multiple ideas can be acted on faster than ever before. You would have immediate access to people and teams who would willingly serve your agenda. You would have access to budgets and assets and capabilities. You would have influence in your industry, and even with national and international government, depending on the size of your organization. In the world of politics, we need look no further than the example of the US President JFK's future shaping mission 'To put a man on the Moon by end of the decade' to show what can be achieved when a leader is in a position of immense power and influence. With the right platform, there may be no limit to what you can make happen.

As an aside, it is also worth noting that unfortunately many top leaders and CEOs do not use their platform for all that could be achieved during their window of power – because they tend to define their domain of responsibility too narrowly. They think only about the financial optics and quarterly targets, and forget to rise above the detail and be more creative about the outcomes they could achieve.

It is definitely easier and faster to get things done when you have positional power. However, positional power is not the only route to having a powerful platform. You can enhance your personal power by being an expert in your field (ie expert power), and by being trusted and respected by others for who you are, what you stand for, how you behave under pressure (ie referent power). You can expand your expert power at any level in the organization by investing time and effort in mastering your chosen niche or topic or technical area. You can grow your referent power in any role, and at any level, by doing your job well, handling yourself well, and being reliable and consistent on performance and results. Depending on your current reputation, you may already have more personal power than you first realized. By expanding your personal power, you will greatly help accelerate and intensify your leadership impact along to the path to more positional power.

Although not mutually exclusive, personal power is arguably a stronger and more inspiring motivator for your followers than positional power. In the examples in Table 7.1, we can see that positional power may not be about true followership, and instead is just a reward contract – or worse, it can tip into coercion.

TABLE 7.1 Positional and personal power

Examples of positional power	Examples of personal power
Legitimate 'I am the CEO or member of the top leadership team so I have authority to set direction, and employees recognize this.'	**Expert** 'I have the skills, knowledge and experience to be best in my field and people recognize this.'
Reward 'I am the boss. Do what I say and I will reward you.'	**Referent** 'I am trusted and respected by others for what I do, who I am, what I stand for and how I handle situations.'
Coercive 'I am the boss. Do what I say or I will fire you.'	**Self-belief** 'I believe in myself and my potential. I am not to be underestimated because I have the core self-confidence to succeed.'

Your reputation is what others say about you – and although you can't control what other people say, you do have a determining hand in what they notice about you. We control what we do and what we say. We control how we behave and, as a result, how others see us. Reputation is not something that just happens, nor is it something that we should leave to chance (Sherman, 2013). Your behaviours, your words, your character or lack of, your strengths, your weaknesses, all add to flavour to the cooking pot of 'reputation'. It could be argued that your reputation is your most important leadership asset – so be mindful of this, and forge your reputation thoughtfully. Trust and reputation are closely linked. You will not have the type of reputation that you may desire as a leader if others feel that they can't trust you (Sherman, 2013). Do you want to know the real secret to building a good reputation? Become a person who deserves one. Take consistent action that embodies the

It could be argued that your reputation is your most important leadership asset.

characteristics you want others to associate with you. Don't just talk about the importance of teamwork, empowerment and future shaping – live out the characteristics that you want associated with you. Let your actions do all the talking and let others discover the admirable character traits in you.

Even if you feel like you have zero power base or zero built-up reputation because no one is paying any attention to you yet, take inspiration from the young people around you. Think of Greta Thunberg, mentioned earlier in this book as a contemporary example of a future shaper leader. Consider her zero base of power and reputation as merely a schoolchild and look at what she achieved within 12 months. From a lone schoolgirl on a lone strike, Greta is an example of how fast you can grow a global platform using only your personal power and no positional power of any kind to begin with. Driven by authentic personal purpose, and speaking her truth, the world sat up and paid attention to Greta. Still only a schoolgirl, she was nominated for a Nobel Peace Prize in 2019 and invited for talks with presidents and parliaments and the United Nations.

CASE EXAMPLE   How a lack of platform can slow down a brilliant idea

Sanjay was a senior commercial lending manager in a bank. As he went about his business of reviewing who would or would not be eligible for commercial loans, Sanjay had an insight and spotted an opportunity for his bank to improve its culture on commercial lending to entrepreneurs.

The bank was very comfortable lending to bigger businesses, but had zero appetite for funding entrepreneurs. In this era of disruption and fast start-up to IPO, Sanjay thought the bank was missing a huge opportunity. After all, Apple was just a new venture at one point, and now it is a major dominating force in our world. Every successful business was once a start-up, so why should the bank be so risk-averse and downright dismissive of entrepreneurs? Risk, of course, would be an issue but could be managed appropriately.

Sanjay decided his long-term preferable outcome was to transform the risk-averse culture of the bank – or part of the bank - and ultimately incubate an 'entrepreneurial bank for entrepreneurs'. He knew the timeframe would depend on how his idea was received from the outset, and suddenly realized that coming up with the idea is the 'easy part'.

Fuelled by his new-found sense of purpose, Sanjay decided he would offer the idea first to the CEO, and failing any take up, he decided he would set up his own bank. Sanjay was not very well networked, his immediate boss was close to retirement and no longer highly engaged in the future of the business. Sanjay knew the name of the CEO, but he couldn't list the names of the company's leaders at the next level down. How was he going to establish any kind of platform of credibility with his CEO? Who could help him get his ideas heard? Starting his journey to realizing his dream of an 'entrepreneurial bank for entrepreneurs' was hampered by platform. Sanjay felt powerless, like a small cog in the massive machinery of his organization.

As a first step, Sanjay created a tactical plan to figure out the degrees of connection between him and the CEO, to figure out who would introduce him to which person to help criss-cross the relationship divide. Sanjay realized that he should have invested more effort in cultivating a better relationship with his boss, with his boss's boss, and with other influencers in the organization. Now that he had a great idea, he had no platform for discussion. Sanjay realized that everyone would have to warm to him before they would even listen to the idea and help him to present the opportunity to the CEO.

Without any platform whatsoever, other than being an employee of the firm, Sanjay felt he was starting at the bottom of the mountain. However, his insight and his dream of a better future fired him up. He took his first step and began the journey to shaping the future he desired.

Impact – merit alone is not sufficient; ignore politics at your peril

When you establish political will from powerful people for your future shaper preferable, you are more likely to achieve your goals. To build your future shaper platform you will have to engage with the politics of your situation. In fact, it is inevitable that the more platform you build, the more powerful you become and the more you cannot avoid the politics of your situation. They say that just like the top of a mountain, the oxygen is thinner at the top of an organization – and you will have to learn how to sustain yourself at that more competitive level. As a future shaper, you can't ignore the political culture around you. The reality is that corporate politics exist and are normal in any organization or human group. To be a successful future shaper leader you need to be actively alert to the politics and decide how to engage. Ignoring politics is unwise as you can be left blindsided by tactics or agendas more calculated and powerful than your own. Your preferable may have great merit, and be for the highest good of other people; and you may have a motivated team and followership, and be delivering early results. However, if there is no political will by someone powerful enough to block you, and they want to block you, then merit will not matter and all your good plans could be thwarted in service of their agenda.

Ignoring politics or pretending politics do not exist is foolish.

Corporate politics emerge when an individual has their own agenda or interest at heart, without regard for how their action affects the organization or desired outcome. At the expense of others and their objectives, people use manipulation and self-serving behaviours to promote their own interests. Such actions may manifest through power struggles and personal conflicts to obtain power or personal importance.

Ignoring politics or pretending politics do not exist is foolish. The reality is that where there are people, there are politics. Politics is normal. It is just another influencing process and it is important for you to understand how it works and how to use it for the good of your plans and to ensure there are no hidden barriers to the execution of your strategy. We usually hear about politics as a negative and potentially destructive force, but it can also be used in a positive way to help achieve your strategic goals.

When you are lifting your head above the parapet to get ambitious plans under way and executed, pay keen attention to the politics around you. Keenly observe what is happening above and below the surface – the unspoken ecosystem of habits and practices that remain unseen, ie what appears to happening, and what is really going on. Place more value on people's actions over words, ie look at what they do and not what they say. Try to analyse the reasons for political behaviour to unearth their true motivation. Politics is not just negative game-playing. You can play politics for the higher good as well. I like the power and politics model that suggests thinking of those who put their own agenda ahead of everyone else as 'foxes', with the accompanying qualities of cunning and stealth. It suggests comparing people who ignore politics to 'sheep', ie blissfully ignorant of the constant danger they are in from the foxes. Then it goes on to explain that the optimal character in the metaphor is the 'owl', who flies higher, can see the bigger picture and is more knowing than the sheep and wiser than the foxes. The 'owls' of politics rise above and are able to outmanoeuvre the foxes by surfacing their negative intentions, behaviours and agendas.

TABLE 7.2 Four core components of political skill

Political astuteness	This refers to the ability to read others, your organization and yourself.
Political effectiveness	After the read out, knowing what combination of tactics to use, at whom to direct them, choosing the right moment, performing the words and deeds effectively.
Political networking	Establishing carefully nurtured relationships within and beyond your organization, which build your reputation, oil wheels and enable you to press the right buttons when seeking support for your desired outcomes.
Political social skills	The ability to get on with other people, do favours for other people, making you likeable and consequently considered more favourably by others when you need their support.

The future shaper leader must learn to defend themselves against the dark side of politics, and get more skilled at engaging in positive political behaviours at all levels of the organization and ecosystem. Studies show that individuals with political skills tend to do better in gaining more personal power, as well as managing stress, than their politically naïve counterparts. Try to understand the informal networks at play. Identify the key brokers and ally with them, so that you can increase your own influence. Conversely, if the brokers are doing more harm than good, you can try to isolate them by developing a counter-narrative and strengthening connections with other networks (Jarrett, 2017). Understanding the political terrain can help you fight dysfunctional politics. If you need to redirect the energy of a dysfunctional opponent, your best bet is to use either reasoned argument or appeal to their interests. Try to understand the drivers rather than just judge the behaviours.

HOW TO BECOME MORE POLITICALLY SKILLED

Scan your environment and appreciate the context, players and objectives:

- Who could positively or negatively influence my preferable outcome?
- Why would they support/not support my ambitions?
- How well do I know these people? How well do they know me?
- How could I better understand their drivers and motivations?
- How can I demonstrate my interest in them and my respect for their expertise or knowledge?
- How might I be of service to each of these people?

Build alignment and alliances:

- Be open to working with difference and conflicts of interest, not just always trying to find consensus and commonality.

- Actively seeking out new alliances and partnerships.
- Try to bring difficult issues into the open.

Get better at reading people and situations:

- Analyse or intuit the dynamics that might occur when stakeholders and agendas come together.
- Recognize different interests and agendas of people and their organizations.
- Discern the underlying, not just the espoused, agendas.
- Use knowledge of institutions, processes and social systems to understand what is happening or what might happen.

Use your interpersonal skills to influence the thinking and behaviour of others:

- Get buy-in from those over whom you have no direct authority.
- Be ready to negotiate; stand up to pressures from other people; handle conflict in order to achieve constructive outcomes.
- Observe and learn from those who have mastered political astuteness.

Be aware of your own motives and behaviours:

- Exercise self-control; be open to the views of others; listen to others and reflect on and be curious about their views.
- Have a proactive disposition.

Source: adapted from www.open.edu/openlearn/ocw/mod/oucontent/view.php?id=68674&section=4.3

In the final chapter I look at another tactic for expanding your platform, which is to collaborate with other like-minded future shapers. There is more power in numbers, and if you also have a high number of peer-level contacts who openly support you, this can increase your platform and ability to get things done. Leadership doesn't have to be such a lonely sport. Finding your tribe of future shaper peers and senior influencers will increase the power of your mutual platform by standing together, sharing resources and ideas, and doing what it takes to support each other to achieve your goals.

When all your hard work and efforts culminate in achieving a very strong and powerful platform in your organization and beyond, now your leadership life becomes a lot easier. The future shaper fundamentals are easier to apply. You would enjoy less resistance to your ideas when you already have a strong follower-ship, eager to hear your next big idea and ready and willing to help you to achieve it. The sheer effort it takes to bring your preferables into reality can be minimized. You are no longer struggling to try to shape the future you desire. From a position of power and leverage, you are actually able to shape the future. People listen to you. When you get to this enviable state, keep challenging yourself to shape more and more ambitious preferables.

Having achieved a strong platform, now you have even more power to shape the future. Take your window of power and use it well. I encourage you to become more confident and more ambitious as you learn the skills of future shaping. Deliberately cultivate the traits to support the skill of future shaping. In the next part I offer you my perspective on traits that underpin the success of the future shaper leader. I use the acronym F.U.T.U.R.E. S.H.A.P.E.R. as a device and memory aid.

STEPHEN HAWKING – FUTURE SHAPER

Hawking was a future shaper who defied all the odds to build a global influencing platform and make his mark on the world. As a pop-culture icon, Stephen Hawking brought physics to the masses and inspired a generation of physicists, most famously with his book *A Brief History of Time*. Yet in 1963, Hawking was diagnosed with a neurological disease called amyotrophic lateral sclerosis and told he had just two years to live, a prediction that he defied for many decades. Hawking spent much of his life in a wheelchair and needed a computerized speech synthesizer to give him his voice. Despite these limitations, Hawking grew a world stage platform of influence and became a 'rock star' scientist because of his willingness and desire to bring science to popular culture.

On the world stage, Hawking was routinely consulted for insights and predictions on everything from time travel and alien life to Middle Eastern politics and nefarious robots. He had an endearing sense of humour and a daredevil attitude – relatable human traits that, combined with his seemingly superhuman mind, made Hawking a world stage influencer.

Q: What world-changing idea, small or big, would you like to see implemented by humanity?

A: This is easy. I would like to see the development of fusion power to give an unlimited supply of clean energy, and a switch to electric cars. Nuclear fusion would become a practical power source and would provide us with an inexhaustible supply of energy, without pollution or global warming.

Sources: Aron (2018); Hawking (2018)

Key takeaways

- The bigger your platform, the wider your support and reach of influence, the easier it will be for you to shape the future you desire.
- You can build up your platform and power base, even if starting from a low or no base. Leadership has become more democratic and level of seniority is no longer the only source of power. Leadership can come from any level.
- There are many strategies, including more effective networking, regarding what you can do today to amplify your reputation and status and grow more followership.
- Where there are people, there are politics. Get actively engaged in the politics of your situation and learn how to build a groundswell of political will for your preferable outcome.

FUTURE SHAPER FUNDAMENTALS CASE STUDY   'To put a man on the Moon by end of the decade'

Having examined each of the five fundamentals in detail, let's now sense-check them in action against a future-shaping mission that is widely recognized as one of humanity's greatest achievements.

Mankind's most audacious future-shaping mission

To put a man on the Moon by end of the decade.

US PRESIDENT JOHN F KENNEDY, 1961

Arguably, the four companies that mainly shape our lives now are Apple, Amazon, Facebook and Google. You don't have to be a founder and tech entrepreneur to be a future shaper, but when we seek to find examples of contemporary Future Shapers, we tend to think of tech entrepreneur business leaders like Steve Jobs, Jeff Bezos, Mark Zuckerberg, Larry Page and Sergey Brin. We remember the role Microsoft founder Bill Gates played in transforming our use of technology. We would probably also list inventors like the co-founder of Tesla Motors, Elon Musk. While these leaders don't possess all the desired future shaper leadership traits I outline later, there is no doubt that these are the iconic business leaders of today who influence how our world works and consequently shape our tomorrow.

Despite these examples of visionaries, no vision has ever been so legacy-making, so audacious and as imaginative as US President JFK's mission in the 1960s to put a man on the Moon by end of the decade. He set out a clear preferable; he persuaded Congress and the American people to support the mission. He built the Apollo team as a fantastic example of a winning team, who faced incredible challenges, learned from their mistakes and kept on persisting. Unfortunately, due to his untimely death in 1963, JFK was unable to witness the completion of his vision, but it is testimony to his ability to unify the US and its politicians behind the mission that his later successor continued to use the presidential platform to pursue the space programme. In 1969 Neil Armstrong became the first man to walk on the Moon and spoke the unforgettable line 'One small step for man. One giant leap for mankind.'

Let's sense-check five key future shaper levers against this historic mission:

- **Preferable**

Did JFK set out a clear preferable outcome? Yes.

In 1961, 44-year-old John F Kennedy became one of the youngest ever presidents of the United States of America. He beat Nixon to the presidency by one of the smallest margins in US history. Desperate to win over a divided nation, the young president's inaugural speech ended with a now famous phrase that beautifully encapsulated Kennedy's leadership vision and inspiration, 'Ask not what your country can do for you, ask what you can do for your country'. Kennedy's presidency did not start well and he wanted a vision that would engage the hearts and minds of all Americans. After many months of considering ideas and options, the president eventually supported an audacious goal: the world's first manned mission to the Moon. Mindful of the Russians beating the US to the punch, Kennedy added a tough time frame, declaring that he wanted a man to walk on the Moon before the end of the decade.

Notice how JFK set out a purposeful, legacy-making, imaginative and clearly defined preferable – to put a man on the Moon by end of this decade. Notice his future shaper traits of fearlessness of ambition and his talented leadership ability to unify all political parties and the country behind his mission.

- **Persuasion**

Did JFK need to persuade stakeholders and budget holders? Yes.

Even the most powerful man in the US had to figure out how to persuade his stakeholders and budget holders to resource his plans. Getting to the Moon was going to cost a fortune and Kennedy had to first convince Congress that this was a prize worth paying for. In May 1961, Kennedy appeared before a joint session of Congress to deliver a special message on 'urgent national needs'. He outlined his spectacular vision, which would involve immense technological challenges, and an eye-watering budget of $7–$9 billion (in reality the programme eventually cost $25 billion!). The president declared that all of the US was going to have to work together if this audacious goal were to stand any chance of success. For Kennedy, this was not about sending one person to the Moon, but rather an entire nation reaching for the stars. The president was concerned that Congress might reject his proposal or be tempted to commit to a much smaller spend, but his brave and bold vision won the day. I have no doubt that there was significant investment in pre-meetings and lobbying key influencers in advance, because the motion was carried after just one hour of debate.

In just a few short months, the president had managed to motivate politicians, the public, scientists and engineers alike. The US had found its dream destination and humanity was on its way to the Moon.

Notice JFK's talent for persuasion – his ability to inspire, his ability to create followership, his ability to convince the budget holders; and notice the supporting leadership traits – fearlessness, unifying, persuasive and energizing.

- **Persistence**

Did the Apollo mission leaders meet any obstacles, and persist to achieve the preferable? Yes.

On the day John F Kennedy was shot, the Apollo Mission lost its leader and key sponsor. But such was the level of buy in and desire from the public to see his legacy through, the mission continued. Under JFK's leadership, and subsequently under President Nixon's tenure, major problems emerged during the Apollo programme – technological challenges, mistakes made, a tragic fire resulting in loss of life and an understandable dip in morale, hard lessons learned and a renewal of Apollo's culture, all fascinatingly documented in Mission Control member Gene Kranz's book *Failure Is Not an Option*. The politicians continued to provide Apollo with the support and financial resources necessary to complete the mission. Apollo 8 was a huge success and by then, the Apollo team had just one year to meet Kennedy's deadline of having a person step onto the lunar surface before the decade was out.

- **Prove**

Was the Apollo team high performing and did they prove successful with their mission and deliver the preferable? Yes.

On 20 July 1969, Neil Armstrong became the first person to walk on the Moon.

Critical to success of the mission was the recruitment of the Apollo team. Team members came from a modest background, and were used to working hard and overcoming adversity. People chosen were optimistic and passionate about putting a man on the Moon, and – interestingly – were deliberately chosen so young so that they didn't realize the task was virtually impossible. Their mindset was uncluttered, unhesitant and totally open to possibilities. Apollo engineer and early team member, Jerry Bostick, captured the driving spirit and culture of the team when he explained 'The President had set out a really clear goal in a single sentence, and it was up to us to make it happen'.

Notice the team was not made up of ivory tower scientists, but hard-working people who were inspired by their leader and truly believed in their mission. There was a certain genius in building a high-performing team of people who didn't realize such a mission was virtually impossible. Removing mindset barriers and believing in the impossible is what shapes and transforms the future. Putting a man on the Moon was a breakthrough future shaping leadership act – reshaping the future for all mankind, for always, and accelerating technological advances as man pushed forward to new frontiers.

- **Platform**

Did the President of the United States of America have the right platform? Heck, yes!

Of course, as President of United States of America, JFK – and later President Nixon – had a pretty powerful platform to bring his preferable into the future. It was such a bold mission and is an example of how, without such a platform, such an expensive and audacious outcome would never have come to pass. Platform is crucial. We can't all be president, but we can all dream big – and we can all invest in building our platform to give our dreams the best shot of becoming a future reality.

The moon landing was a very remarkable future shaping feat. This achievement resembles the moment Christopher Columbus first set foot on the shores of America, but instead of setting foot on the sands of a new-found country, Armstrong stepped onto the soil of a new *world*. This event was crucial in the heart of mankind; it unified the world in a way nothing else could because we knew, as humankind, that the impossible had been accomplished. Even Richard Nixon, who was US president at the time said: 'For one priceless moment, all the people on Earth are truly one'. This event is also very influential in the development of our present society; it is a message to all that mankind can and will accomplish anything. It truly was one small step for man, and a giant leap for all mankind.

Source: some text adapted from Wiseman (2019)

PART FOUR

Future shaper leadership intelligence traits

CHAPTER EIGHT

F.U.T.U.R.E. shaper leadership traits

FIGURE 8.1   F.U.T.U.R.E.

Fearless: *unhampered by self-doubts, bold and brave decision making*

Empathetic: *ability to appreciate the other person's context and understand their feelings*

Unconventional: *creative and not conforming to what is generally done or believed*

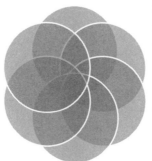

Resilient: *a capacity to withstand or recover quickly from difficult conditions*

Tenacious: *a dogged determination to achieve key outcomes and not easily discouraged*

Unifying: *skilled in how to bring diverse groups together to pursue common goals*

I t may seem like a stretch to possess all the desired future shaper leadership traits. I encourage you to start by absorbing the information and use this first list of six traits to form an impression of the kind of leadership traits you need to aspire to, and to cultivate to be a future shaper. Check which one speaks to you the most. Which one really resonates, and why? Which one really challenges you, and why? Think about whether it would have been an entirely different set of words five or even two years ago. It makes sense that a different global landscape and changed business climate requires a radical shift in new traits required.

✓ **Be Fearless:** courage is about feel the fear and do it anyway. Fearlessness is about having no fear at all. Imagine that.

✓ **Be Unconventional:** a lack of concern with conformity in order to free up your creative mind and unleash more innovative ideas.

✓ **Be Tenacious:** the tenacious leader never quits. They never give up, and just keep on going in service of their vision and their people and results. They will always find a way forward.

✓ **Be Unifying:** unifying is bigger than collaboration; it is about bringing people together – including the ability to reach out to disparate groups and include them in the common goal.

✓ **Be Resilient:** resilience is your capacity to withstand and recover quickly from difficult conditions. Tenacity is about never quitting and resilience is about your ability to endure shocks and setbacks.

✓ **Be Empathetic:** being empathetic is about being able to understand and share the feelings of another. It is a key element in emotional intelligence, the link between self and others.

These are all traits that can be cultivated. Please don't be intimidated by this list. It is better to set a high standard for future shapers and empower you to reach for it; than to set the bar too low and underestimate your potential.

Be Fearless

Uncertain times require bold, confident, fearless leadership. The future shaper leader confronts reality head-on, says what needs to be said, does what needs to be done – and holds themselves and their people accountable for the results. Fearlessness is one step beyond courage. Courage is about feel the fear and do it anyway. Fearlessness is about having no fear at all. Imagine that? It would be truly liberating for leadership decision-making. When we gaze into the future, there is an excitement about possibilities but in truth, most of us are fear-led. Fear makes us self-conscious, afraid of doing the wrong thing, afraid of upsetting people, afraid of making mistakes. All of which prevents us from moving forward in a constructive way. All of which stop us from being great leaders. We would be better decision makers if fear was not clouding our judgement. If you doubt yourself, you second guess your next move. Your fear may be sabotaging your great ideas. Fear stops us from achieving our leadership goals.

Fear makes us self-conscious, afraid of doing the wrong thing, afraid of upsetting people, afraid of making mistakes

We live in interesting times and we face inevitable shocks, setbacks and failures. The fearless future shaper already knows this, acknowledges it, and is willing to push aside their fear of the unknown and keep moving forward. The future shaper has the guts to say 'let's go this way' and has the fearlessness to bring people with them, and course-correct as new forces impact on strategic decision-making. The fearless future shaper is ready to take risks and stand behind difficult decisions, which may be as drastic as 'if we don't do this, the business may not survive'.

Fearlessness is the trait you need to cultivate initially for the 'preferable' component of the future shaper formula. When you are setting out your preferable, don't let fear hold back your ambition. Be fearless about what you want to manifest, and go for it! Fearlessness is also a key trait necessary to cultivate for persistence. During testing times, you have to trust yourself and trust that you will overcome all obstacles.

Whilst not having all the traits of a future shaper, Jeff Bezos is a good example of a leader who has exhibited the trait of fearlessness during his career. Despite many challenges and multiple setbacks, he has always fearlessly pushed forward – and is now even going beyond earthly business ventures to find new business frontiers in outer space:

- Can you practise letting go of fear?
- Are you good at stepping back to gain a better perspective?
- Are you ready to step up and step out of your comfort zone?
- Are you willing to make fearless business decisions and take more risks?

TECHNIQUES FOR CULTIVATING FEARLESSNESS

✓ Take more risks. Go after what you want.

✓ Speak up. Let others know what you stand for.

✓ Get out of your comfort zone. Do the things you are afraid of.

✓ Practise making decisions without any fear of negative consequences.

✓ Embrace change, including what may seem to be negative change, as a learning opportunity.

✓ When things go wrong, don't overreact. Learn to trust yourself and trust that everything will work out. There is a solution for everything.

✓ Ask yourself 'What is the worst that could happen?', make your peace with that, then liberate yourself to act.

✓ Remind yourself that the outcomes you want to achieve for the future are more important than the fear you feel today.

✓ Don't be afraid to fail. Don't let fear control you or drive your decision making. Be open to learning from failure and try again.

Reflective exercise: Write down all the things that you fear and are holding you back from achieving your preferable outcomes. Visualize a fire: throw your fears into the fire and watch them burn one by one. You have the power to choose not to be afraid of some imaginary future that has not yet happened. Stay in the moment, and let go of fear. Have faith in yourself and your ambitions.

Be Unconventional

I am good at thinking outside the box, so much that you realize it's not a box to begin with.

WILL.I.AM – FUTURE SHAPER

Linked to fearlessness is feeling liberated to stand up for what you believe in and being prepared to challenge the status quo. Being unconventional is about not conforming to what is generally done or believed. By definition the disruptor is unconventional. Don't be afraid to go against the grain. Your idea may be the opposite of what everyone else is thinking and doing but this is how great innovation seeds; someone sees the glimpse of an alternative way of doing something and spots an opportunity to plug a gap in the market. Try to cultivate a lack of concern with conformity in order to free up your creative mind and unleash more innovative ideas.

It always feels easier and less confrontational to fit in – but think about the inherent losses and opportunity cost of this attitude. Unconcerned by what other people think of them, the unconventional thinker can bring a unique edge and idea that may make all the difference to how to go to market. The unconventional leader frees themselves from any concern for mistakes or ridicule. They see failed attempts as building blocks towards greater success. You don't have to lead the way other people expect you to – do it your own way. Behaving differently may wrong-foot your opponents. Don't say to yourself 'well I am just not unconventional' as if that's that and you can't change. Retrain your brain. You can learn to be more unconventional by cultivating this trait as a new habit. For example, think of a current issue you are facing and ask yourself 'what would be an unconventional approach to this situation that would add value?' Put 'first, break all the rules' as a mantra at the forefront of your thinking when you want to be more creative or when you are problem solving – and see what alternative ideas and options you develop. Is there something in your business and industry that just does not work for customers any more? Are people tired of paying 'hidden' extra charges, and jaded from poor customer service? Is there is a 'better, faster, cheaper' alternative to be created that can get your customers excited again and disrupt your industry status quo? When an unconventional leader hears 'it has never been done this way before' they get excited. Try to adopt this same response as a new habit for yourself.

Developing an unconventional streak will really help you with ideating your preferred future outcome and exploring ideas on what the future could look like. It will also change how you recruit your teams and 'prove' better results. Unconventional leaders proactively build diverse teams around them that challenge the old and reinvent the new. They go outside of their comfort zone; they intentionally seek diversity of opinions, ages, genders, perspectives, experiences. They don't want to build an army of 'yes' men and women, they want to innovate and evolve. It is difficult to manage a team of 'rebels' but the unconventional leader knows that is exactly what is needed to change the norm:

- Are you willing to think differently, experiment and innovate?
- Can you suspend belief in how things are, and question your basic assumptions?
- Are you open to ideas from alternative sources, and trying out new 'unlikely' approaches?

TECHNIQUES FOR CULTIVATING UNCONVENTIONALITY

✓ Stay open to all possibilities.

✓ Be comfortable with non-conforming.

✓ Practise trusting your instincts rather than following the crowd.

✓ Become more curious by asking 'why?' and 'why not?' more often.

✓ Invite differences of opinions, ask people to challenge your ideas.

✓ Recruit people from diverse backgrounds and experiences on to your team.

✓ Accept yourself, your differences, value your alternative point of view.

✓ Get out of your echo chamber, ie the environment in which you encounter only beliefs or opinions that coincide with your own, so that your existing views are reinforced and alternative ideas are not considered.

Reflective exercise: Reflect on the types of leaders you admire most – past or present. Do these people demonstrate any unconventional character traits? What are they, and why did it make such an impact on you?

Be Tenacious

Tenacity is a common attribute of the most successful people and vital for future shaper leadership. It's often one of the key missing ingredients of chronic underachievers. You could be fearless and unconventional, with the most creative vision and plan, but you also need the ability to stick with it and drive it to a successful conclusion if you want to be a successful future shaper. In today's volatile world, what our leaders need is a high level of tenacity to deliver on their vision. They also need to be very comfortable in dealing with ambiguity and leading through long periods of organizational and industry uncertainty.

Tenacity is about not readily relinquishing a position, principle or course of action. In this context it is about having a vision of the future, and persisting and persevering in service of key determined outcomes. There is an old saying: 'do not judge someone by how many times they have been knocked down, judge them by how many times they have got back up'. The tenacious leader never quits. They will never give up, and will just keep going in service of their vision and their people and results. They will always find a way to keep showing up and keep going on their mission.

The refusal to give up and the ability to keep going is what successful people do. They develop the mental toughness to keep going when the average person would reasonably quit. This is not easy to do, especially depending on how big the obstacle or setback. But it can be learned. Project setbacks, technical challenges, resource issues or political roadblocks are not reasons to give up. Leader, this is where you earn your keep! The more you focus on the positive, the better your mind will get at moving on and the more tenacious you will become. Your level of tenacity can improve and is developed over time. Mental toughness develops by overcoming adversity time and time again. Of course, tenacity itself it is not enough – ultimately the quality of the results of all that tenacity is what matters. We don't get free passes and gold stars for trying hard and failing. Perhaps your level of tenacity is the litmus test for whether you really believe in your preferred outcome. If your vision is really so important, then your level of tenacity will rise accordingly.

Cultivating the trait of tenacity is critical for the 'persist' component of the future shaper framework. It is also important for 'prove' component and having the staying power to drive out the results required:

- Do you have a tendency to quit too easily, when the going gets tough?
- Do you have the grit, stamina and staying power to stick with your vision?
- Is your preferred future outcome worth investing all this energy?

TECHNIQUES FOR CULTIVATING TENACITY

✓ Practise optimism – tenacity dies when hope dies.

✓ Practise never giving up on your dreams – it is a conscious choice to not quit.

✓ Capture and record the successes – to sustain yourself and your people on the journey.

✓ Identify your personal role models, who have achieved greatness and just kept on going, despite all the odds. Let them inspire you.

✓ It is hard to stay motivated and positive 100 per cent of the time, so surround yourself with motivated people who can carry the torch for you, when necessary.

✓ Be crystal clear on your purpose and the outcomes you want to achieve; the anticipation that you might make a difference energizes tenacity.

✓ Keep a healthy perspective on problems and don't catastrophize setbacks. Stay focused on the bigger picture and resolve to try again, by applying new ideas and approaches.

✓ Notice people who are tenacious – at work, or on the sports field – and emulate their strategies; why are they so determined, why are they undeterred, what drives them, how can you learn from them?

Reflective exercise: Consider who or what you rely upon as your foundation of strength and source of support. What stabilizes you when the going gets tough? Consider how to better appreciate and nurture these sources of sustenance, as they are fuelling your ability to stay tenacious.

Be **U**nifying

The unifying trait is about bringing people together – including the ability to reach out to disparate groups and include them in the pursuit of your common goal. You will have been lectured many times on the importance of collaboration. But in my view, 'unifying' is a stronger leadership trait than being collaborative. Yes, of course you must learn to collaborate and work with people to get things done, but to go that step further and unify people is at another more special leadership level.

The unifying leader should be able to take everyone's ideas into consideration, influence others and settle disputes. Unifying leadership is about the ability to work across borders – functional, organizational, cultural and social. It is about how to pull people together from different areas or silos of the business, and inspire them with a meaningful purpose and vision, encouraging sharing and teamwork in order to produce great results. Success comes when everyone achieves a desired goal together. You may need to be able to assemble multiple teams to work effectively together, knowing when to invite and connect the right people into the effort. You will need to empathize and influence using win–win appeals and proposals. You also need to be able to recognize when unification and collaboration is working versus when it has tipped into endless meetings, debating ideas and struggling to find consensus. Don't confuse unifying with consensus building. Consensus building often grinds decision making and execution to a halt. The ability to unify people is much more strategic than that!

'UNITED WE STAND, DIVIDED WE FALL'

Aesop's fable: The Four Oxen and the Lion

A lion used to prowl about a field in which four oxen used to dwell. Many a time he tried to attack them; but whenever he

---

came near they turned their tails to one another, so that whichever way he approached them he was met by the horns of one of them. At last, however, they fell a-quarrelling among themselves, and each went off to pasture alone in a separate corner of the field. Then the lion attacked them one by one and soon made an end of all four.

Breaking down silos and unifying people behind a cause that inspires them can make a transformative difference to any desired outcome. Try to find a way for people to get out of their small group, because small thinking mentality operates at the expense of the greater good. Unifying people and compelling them to set aside their differences in favour of a greater cause may sound impossible at first – however the first step is to observe and identify divisions and then resolve to break down cliques and siloed thinking. You need to bring people to a greater understanding of what matters and why.

Cultivating the trait of 'unifying' is important for the 'persuade', 'persist' and 'platform' elements of the future shaper formula. Your ability to unify people around a common desired future outcome will make or break your leadership success as a future shaper. Without a shared vision there is no foundation, motivation, direction or focus for the team. It is simply a working group of individuals whose energies are all directed towards their individual roles and responsibilities.

A unifying vision builds strength and optimizes effort; creates concentration; generates cooperation; reduces frustration; helps resolve conflict; assists evaluation. The shared vision becomes a meaningful standard against which to promote unity and resolve clashes between the interests of the individual and the greater good:

- Do you approach tasks with a unifying mindset?
- Are you able to bring people together under a shared vision and mission?
- Are you expansive about the definition of stakeholders and are you inclusive of all communities, and do you seek to find common goals?

TECHNIQUES FOR CULTIVATING UNIFYING CAPABILITY

✓ Provide clear and understandable goals.

✓ Establish a shared mission and communicate it regularly.

✓ Involve your team and stakeholders in decision making.

✓ Seek out the mutual benefits and 'win–win' scenarios – so that your vision becomes 'our' vision.

✓ Language is important – be mindful of the words you use as they can either powerfully unify or powerfully alienate other people.

✓ Expand your definition of who constitutes a stakeholder of your preferable – beyond the obvious – and try to understand all their interests and motivations.

✓ Be a good communicator because lack of communication leads to fear, anger and disunity. Be a voice for the voiceless – mindful that some people may not feel that they have any power in the team or stakeholder group.

✓ Foster relationships across borders. Notice when cliques and divisions emerge – and remind everyone of the higher goal to be served. Pay attention to your own behaviour and don't ever 'take sides'.

Be Resilient

Resilience is like a first cousin of tenacity. Tenacity is about never quitting and resilience is about your ability to endure. Together they combine to provide you with the kind of robustness and strength of spirit and capability to be successful as a future shaper.

Resilience is necessary for the future shaper leader because leading in uncertain times requires someone with the capacity to withstand trials and tribulations, and renew themselves again and again in the face of any overwhelm, negativity, and persistent blocks and challenges at every twist and turn. Resilience is a critical component of the energy needed for stepping up to be a future shaper. Optimism is crucial to resilience. When faced with negative experiences, you will need to see the glass half full.

Future shaper leadership resilience is all about endurance and moving forward in spite of setbacks and adversity, with a robust capacity to:

- recover from setbacks;
- tolerate adversity, ambiguity and stress;
- bounce back from challenges and change;
- act positively and assertively in difficult situations;
- keep moving forward with strength.

Even in more stable times, life and work were never all smooth sailing. However, with a new context of uncertain times, the importance of having resilience gets dialled right up. In uncertain and unpredictable times, major changes occur, such as more buyouts, takeovers, forced redundancies, and having to do more with less budget and fewer resources. The question is how resilient you are as a leader at avoiding, anticipating and bouncing back from setbacks in the face of all the disruption and uncertainty in today's world.

The resilient leader is able to stay focused and centred on the most important priorities, even when all the odds seem stacked against them. The resilient leader endures, renews, adapts. The resilient leader is often quite emotionally intelligent: able to read the situation, calm other people down, able to make a decision when others hesitate, able to be highly present for themselves and for others in the eye of the storm. Resilient leaders are able to remain clear-headed and principled in spite of increasing anxieties and escalating change. I notice that leaders who are very resilient are those that have the capacity to understand but not overreact to an immediate threat; they can receive bad news and stay calm, create options for next steps and make good decisions under pressure.

Resilience is a critical leadership trait to cultivate to support the 'persist' component of the future shaper formula. 'Persist' is the most important element of the formula, and 'resilience' is a must-have leadership trait to survive in the now and in the future:

- How quickly do you recover from setbacks?
- Are you able to handle ambiguity and keep moving forward?
- Are you able to role model your resilience and motivate the troops to be more resilient too?

TECHNIQUES FOR CULTIVATING RESILIENCE

✓ Stay motivated and focused on what really matters.

✓ Stay strong in self-belief – be confident that you can solve problems.

✓ Grow a thicker skin – accept that everyone makes mistakes, no one is perfect.

✓ Talk about the issues – problems seem less insurmountable once we voice them.

✓ Ask for help; don't try to be a hero. Open up and solicit ideas from the perspective of others.

✓ Sit with discomfort – sometimes it's a matter of waiting it out, until a difficult phase passes.

✓ Self-talk and mantras can be really helpful in stressful situations, eg 'This too shall pass', 'There is always a solution', 'Does this really matter?'

✓ Develop techniques for replenishing your physical and emotional energy. For some it's about physical fitness, eating and sleeping well, staying grounded through family and friends, and having an enriching life outside work.

✓ Take detachment breaks – daily and weekly, and take any holidays you are due. When we step away from work and take a break, even for a few minutes, it allows our brain activity to settle down and we can reset our energy and attention.

Reflective exercise: Describe a time when you led with conviction. What was your goal? What were you standing for? Why did it matter? What challenges faced you and how did you overcome? How resilient did you need to be? Did you achieve the desired outcome? Why/why not?

Be Empathetic

Leadership is, of course, a very human and social process. Without other people following, you cannot lead. The future shaper leader needs to be able to relate to others and to be relatable. This speaks to how you tune in to the emotional life of your team, your stakeholders, the company culture, the atmosphere in the room – and it can lead to new more meaningful ways to motivate your team, people and followers. The more in tune you are with the feelings and mood of the people around you, the more informed you are about their concerns, motivations and goals, the better your leadership decisions.

Being empathetic is about being able to put yourself in the other person's shoes – allowing you greater insight on how they feel about the task, your decision, the goal or issue, or whatever arises. It is a key element in emotional intelligence, the link between self and others, because it is how we as individuals understand what others are experiencing as if we were feeling it ourselves.

Some people misunderstand the word 'empathy' and perceive it to be a weak position; they confuse it with 'sympathy' and think it is just about being nice to people, making cups of tea, mopping tears and getting people to like you. The other extreme is the hard-nosed business leader who doesn't value the role of empathy, who just wants to get the job done, and never takes into account the impact on others. Yes, it is about getting the job done; however, by being empathetic you may become more creative about the solution, or you may unlock what is stopping the other person from completing the task successfully. It is no longer realistic to tell others what to do and expect them to jump to our command. This kind of authoritarian command and control leadership approach may work short term, or in a crisis, but it does not work with people over the long term. Your team and workforce seek to be engaged, motivated and inspired to strive and support you in your goals. Empathy is not sympathy. It does not mean you have to agree with how someone is feeling, or even relate to their feelings. Instead, empathy is all about the awareness of other people's feelings and making that connection. Empathy means you are able to then apply that awareness of another's feelings, and understand how it affects their needs.

In the era of increasing artificial intelligence, improved emotional intelligence will serve the future shaper leader very well.

I would like to add that although leadership is definitely not a popularity contest, I have noticed that if people both respect and like you then they will work harder for you. Empathy is the emotional currency for building better bonds and better trust with your team and others. In the era of increasing artificial intelligence, improved emotional intelligence will serve the future shaper leader very well.

Empathy is a very important trait underpinning the 'persuade' component of the future shaper formula. When it comes to negotiating what you want, you will need to understand what other people want, and how to find common ground and set up mutual wins. Negotiation is not always about rational logic, it is also about understanding the emotional needs at play during the deal:

- Are you a good listener?
- Are you in tune with people and events?
- Do your decisions take into account the feelings, needs and motivation of other people?

TECHNIQUES FOR CULTIVATING EMPATHY

✓ Be open to incorporating the views of others.

✓ Try to tune in to the emotions and feelings of others.

✓ Develop a habit of asking yourself what the other person would do.

✓ Take the time to consider how your actions might impact how other people feel.

✓ Establish structures and space to encourage other people to fully share their views.

✓ Park your viewpoint and try to see the situation from the other person's point of view.

✓ Listen intelligently. What is being said, and what is being left unsaid but is also important to hear?

✓ Respond encouragingly when someone is struggling to communicate with you, so that they are able to better express their views to you, and you are able to hear them.

✓ Challenge your own prejudice – your own bias and assumptions. See beyond labels, or preconceptions of the other person or group.

✓ We all share the same human experience; we all have more in common with each other than we have differences. Remember this when you are trying to connect with people you don't necessarily like or agree with.

I hope you really connect with this F.U.T.U.R.E. list and will make a conscious effort and commitment to personal change and evolution – for your benefit and the benefit of all those around you, who look to you, the leader, as a role model and example of how to behave. The F.U.T.U.R.E. list is the first half of a blueprint to help transform you into a future shaper leadership way of being. If you really want to adopt these traits, you need to practise them in your leadership life, notice what works or what doesn't work. Through practice and experience you will embed these traits into your leadership genetic code.

Having examined the F.U.T.U.R.E. traits, let's now move on to the next chapter to explore the S.H.A.P.E.R. traits, which are the second half of the leadership blueprint that you will need to cultivate to be a true future shaper leader.

CHAPTER NINE

Future S.H.A.P.E.R. leadership traits

FIGURE 9.1   S.H.A.P.E.R.

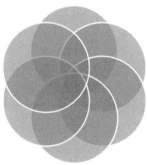

Super-adaptable: *an impressive agility and ability to adjust quickly to new conditions*

Resourceful: *a talent for finding quick and clever ways to overcome difficulties*

Hard-working: *a discipline for tending to work with energy, commitment and diligence*

Energizing: *ability to boost vitality, enthusiasm and energy in others*

Authentic: *genuine in approach and not acting or performing the role of leader*

Proactive: *initiating or making things happen instead of waiting and responding later*

In addition to the F.U.T.U.R.E. traits of the previous chapter, let's discuss six more. I am staying with the device of using an appropriate acronym as a helpful memory aid for what you need to focus on cultivating to be a successful future shaper.

✓ **Be Super-adaptable:** being adaptable is about the ability to react to changes in your environment. In today's shape-shifting world, the future shaper leader needs to be super-adaptable.

✓ **Be Hard-working:** this is about your work ethic, self-discipline and associated qualities of determination, attentiveness, responsibility, problem-solving and self-control.

✓ **Be Authentic:** Authenticity is important because it is about connecting with others. This is not via a performance of how a leader should be, nor the carefully curated version of yourself, designed only to impress. It is about real you – your real personality, your strengths and your flaws.

✓ **Be Proactive:** being proactive is about taking charge of your situation. It is about taking control of your work, your attitude, your destiny and shaping the future. Stop waiting, start creating.

✓ **Be Energizing:** the ability to transmit energy to others starts with feeling passionate about your purpose and role and what you want to achieve. It is about being positive and optimistic and spreading that emotion virally and energetically to your team.

✓ **Be Resourceful:** resourcefulness is about the creative ability to overcome problems and making do with what is available to develop a solution.

Remember that these are all traits that can be cultivated. Please don't be intimidated by this list. It is better to set a high standard for future shapers and empower you to reach for it; than to set the bar too low and underestimate your potential.

Be Super-adaptable

Being adaptable is about the ability to react to changes in your environment. As with the survival of any species, the most successful leaders are those who will adapt fastest to their changing environment.

What worked in the past, or even last year, may not work now. Unpredictability is the new predictability in today's world. Your capacity for responsive, agile thinking and decision making will be crucial for business success. The future shaper leader needs to be flexible and adaptable. Ever nimble, ever quick-thinking, the super-adaptable leader is able to look at an issue from several perspectives, and create a range of alternative solutions before deciding which one best suits the situation.

When the world is in a constant state of flux, the future shaper leader needs to be super-adaptable.

When the world is in a constant state of flux, the future shaper leader needs to be super-adaptable. How good are you at responding and at continuing to make progress when major change occurs? Whether that is at your organization level, such as a company restructure, or in response to major industry change due to technology and digital innovation. The super-adaptable future shaper is constantly horizon-scanning to anticipate what is around the next corner, or next timeline, and assessing if any plans need to change accordingly. You may not always be able to anticipate the change, but you can still handle it when it arrives – because you have established a capacity to be flexible in your environment. Rather than resist change, you expect it, you accept it and you may even embrace it. The super-adaptables are also very good at motivating their team, facilitating change and helping people to achieve their desired outcomes.

The super-adaptable leader is better able to:

- Handle work stress.
- Solve problems creatively.
- Display cultural adaptability.
- Demonstrate interpersonal adaptability.
- Handle emergencies and crisis situations.
- Learn new work tasks, technologies and procedures.
- Deal effectively with unpredictable or changing work situations.

Being super-adaptable is about being super-ready for change. While you may have your preferred future outcome and a competent strategy to reach it, the path that you plan to take should not be set in stone. This allows flexible appropriate responses to the demands of the moment and any detours or unforeseen circumstances are better handled – emotionally and practically.

Being super-adaptable will help you mainly with the 'persist' element of the future shaper formula. It will also help you and your team to course-correct as necessary in order to prove the right results:

- How flexible and adaptable are you to change?
- Are you comfortable with constant horizon-scanning and course-correcting?
- How fast can you renew the strategy and adjust the plan based on new information?
- Can you cope, adapt and assimilate when you find yourself outside your comfort zone?

TECHNIQUES FOR CULTIVATING SUPER-ADAPTABILITY

✓ Welcome opportunities to lead through change or crisis.

✓ Be an early adopter of new ideas. Rather than resist change, be the first one to embrace it.

✓ Gain as much experience as possible on leading international, multicultural teams – a diversity of people, culture and values.

✓ Be open to leading business incubation opportunities to see what it takes to bring an idea from seed to start-up to fruition.

✓ Think outside the box; do you refer to standard operating procedure on everything? Try new and different approaches. Be open to experimenting to find new solutions to new and old problems.

✓ Don't feel under pressure to continually reinvent wheels – instead consider doing the new and unexpected with what you already have, and encourage other people to do the same.

✓ Raise your self-awareness of being too inflexible, too rigid when it comes to your schedule, your needs, your approaches – and introduce a new openness to spontaneity and willingness to change the plan quickly if it is not working.

✓ Embrace the concept of 'modification' – in other words expect and anticipate the need to modify your answer, your path, your plan. Talk about it as an advantage – enabling faster decision making because we can chart a course of action and modify as necessary.

Be Hard-working

It's not that I'm so smart. It's just that I stay with problems longer.

ALBERT EINSTEIN – FUTURE SHAPER

Having the self-discipline to work hard to achieve what you want is crucial to success as a future shaper leader. The ability to get things done and push harder than anyone else is vital if you're going to succeed at anything.

When I think about what it means to be hard-working, I think about the associated qualities of determination, attentiveness, responsibility, problem-solving and self-control. It's about a strong work ethic and a discipline for execution – doing what you need to do, rather than what you want to do, at times. Your work ethic is the way in which you approach your role day to day. It is vital to have a good work ethic to be able to cope with overwhelm and constant challenges. Diligent habits and practices serve us well as we strive to achieve our desired future. The good news is that people who are driven towards their goal are fuelled by their intrinsic passion and motivation – so they enjoy their hard work and it does not seem unduly gruelling to them. They are proud of their efforts, and confident that the destination is worth the journey.

What fuels the hard worker is a work ethic driven by a purpose and desire to achieve their goals. When you begin to work hard towards achieving success, make sure to work smart too – set clear priorities, stay focused on them and don't burn out. You will need to find the optimum balance between working full steam ahead, and knowing when it becomes counter-productive because of tiredness. When you feel tired, remember to take a break, renew and refuel. An intelligent working technique, along with a strong work ethic, will go a long way and will set you apart from your peers.

We all like to take shortcuts, where possible – and you should always stay alert to opportunities to be more nimble and get the job done faster – but sometimes there is no shortcut and then the discipline and commitment from a focused, hard-working approach will differentiate us from those who only want a free and easy pass when the going gets tough. There are many people who coast through their working day, cutting corners and just about getting away with it – these are also the folks who won't survive long in leadership positions when the pressure is turned up.

Being a hard worker will support you in the 'persist' component of the future shaper formula. It will also help you and your team to prove your results. In the end, every achievement is a result of hard work and effort invested – it's the price you pay to get off the starting blocks, run the race and cross the finish line:

- Do you have a strong work ethic?
- Do you enjoy the stretch challenge in working hard to achieve your goals?
- Are you prepared to work hard, push through and put in the extra hours when necessary?

TECHNIQUES FOR BEING MORE HARD-WORKING

✓ Set out your key priorities and stick to them.

✓ Develop the habit of good self-discipline day to day – to build your work ethic 'muscle'.

✓ Celebrate your successes and milestones along the way, to keep your motivation levels up and sustain your morale.

✓ Be willing to put in more effort when necessary. Don't burn out, but don't shy away from investing extra hours in service of your higher goals.

✓ Don't make excuses or blame other people if things go wrong.

✓ Take responsibility for your actions and be accountable for doing what you said you would do.

✓ Don't be easily defeated if you feel like all your hard work is not paying off – yet. No effort is wasted. Cultivate optimism – and by learning to be optimistic, the extra effort you need to put in to get the result you want will feel like less of an issue.

Be **A**uthentic

It is said that we live in a post-truth era. With the proliferation of fake news, false claims, overblown rhetoric and a non-stop stream of information coming from multiple, unknown and layered sources, it's no wonder we have trouble discerning fact from fiction. What we really yearn for amidst all this subterfuge and fakeness, is truthfulness and to be led by authentic leaders. So, added to the fusion of great leadership qualities needed for future shaper leadership today, I encourage you to be your authentic self. I don't mean the carefully curated version of you designed to impress on LinkedIn or Facebook. I mean the real you – your real personality, your best version of you and, of course, your flaws too!

Employees and teams are demanding more authenticity from their leaders in order to feel fully motivated to serve. It is probably a reaction against too many years of anonymous corporations and faceless CEOs telling people what to do. The disillusioned middle ranks are valuing authenticity over claims of 'sincerity' and 'integrity' – which, ironically, they feel are too easily faked. People have an instinct for when somebody is being true to themselves, versus offering us a performance or 'perfection'. We don't want perfection, we all want people who are real, who are aware of their strengths and weaknesses, who will tell it like it is, who will not confuse or patronize.

Just be careful to actually be authentic, rather than try to be authentic. Don't talk about how authentic you are; show how authentic you are through your actions and your behaviour. I notice that when something like 'authentic leadership' becomes a buzzword, then people are happy to parrot the idea without fully exploring what it really means. Authenticity is neither a performance nor a position you can take. It is more about self-awareness and self-expression, being who you really are and doing it your way. Being authentic is about taking off your executive mask and revealing your natural leadership self and true beliefs. It is about appreciating you and your uniqueness, and playing to your natural strengths. As leader, you are in the fortunate position to be able to hire other people who can complement and round out any aspects you lack. When people are faking 'authenticity' it usually shows up eventually when they are in a position of high stress, and that is when their truly authentic character will reveal itself!

Enjoy being liberated from the shackles of some idealized version of what you 'should be' and instead accept how you are. Being authentic is not about straining and forcing – it is about acceptance of how things really are, of how you really are. This honesty is a bedrock for better relationships with your people and teams; it promotes better communication, grows deeper trust and positively impacts performance.

Being authentic will be super important for the 'preferables' and 'persuade' components of the future shaper formula. If you are authentic on the purpose that drives your preferable outcomes, you will feel very connected and committed to what you want to achieve –and this will come across when you are trying to persuade others to back you, and back your ideas. Authenticity is also important for platform, and building your credibility faster with new contacts:

- Are you wearing an executive mask?
- Are you comfortable in your leadership role skin?
- Is authenticity just another performance for you, or can you bring your real self forward to lead?

TECHNIQUES FOR CULTIVATING AUTHENTICITY

✓ Act in ways that genuinely show how you feel.

✓ Celebrate your differences – it is what makes you unique.

✓ Be comfortable about who you are, and what you stand for

✓ Don't feel that you have to perform a role at work. Be yourself.

✓ Tell the truth. Don't cover up any mistakes – be open, be transparent.

✓ Realize your time to make a leadership impact is limited, so don't waste it living someone else's life.

✓ Express your thoughts and feelings. Be yourself, show your human side. It is okay to show your vulnerability.

✓ Authentic people display a consistent set of values, and don't change their behaviour from one conversation to the next.

✓ Ask people for help when you need it. Genuine people accept that they aren't perfect and ask for help when needed.

Be Proactive

Proactivity or proactive behaviour usually refers to self-initiated behaviour that is anticipatory and often change-oriented. Proactive leaders are alert and able to anticipate future needs and start acting on them immediately, as opposed to passively waiting and reacting too late. Proactivity is about being in the control of the situation, rather than being controlled by it.

Being proactive is about taking action early to accelerate a positive outcome, or to neutralize or avoid a negative one. By thinking about potential issues that could arise and being aware of possible future changes, you'll be able to plan and act accordingly in advance. Every future shaper leader needs to be proactive – alert, anticipative, action-oriented. I like to think of proactivity as being the opposite of procrastination – decisions are taken rather than avoided, action is executed rather than put on hold until more perfect information comes along (it never does!). People who are proactive take ownership of the issues and empower themselves on how to sort out problems. Proactive people are the type of people everyone loves to have as a leader and on their team – there are no unnecessary delays, while people wait for instructions. There is no blame game with proactive people; they just roll up their sleeves and tackle the challenges. They take the initiative and go for it.

Proactive leadership calls for strategic thinking. You need the ability to anticipate change or crisis situations and create plans to meet those challenges. This means focusing more on the big picture and less on the immediate problems. Proactive leaders seek to solve problems for the long and short term. They forward-think, and possess great problem-solving skills. Being proactive eliminates a lot of time wasting and getting stuck in the weeds. A proactive leader anticipates what is going to happen and works accordingly to minimize the effect of the event or to work to take advantage of the event. Don't wait for problems to arise before addressing them, or you will find yourself scuttling from crisis to crisis.

Being proactive means you are willing to take charge and set a course of action, when others may hesitate. The proactive trait is most critical to the prove element of the future shaper formula. It is about being attuned to anticipating any issues and doing what it takes to get things done. Being proactive is what it takes to convert your preferable outcomes and manifesting them into concrete reality. Proactivity is about anticipating the future and acting to shape it. By role modelling and actively encouraging the trait of proactivity, you empower your team to help prove the right results. Everyone is in forward motion, and driving towards the desired preferables:

- Are you good at anticipating problems, changes and contributing plans to overcome?
- Can you spot what is happening at the intersections – of your business, your industry – and are you ready to exploit opportunities for business advantage?
- Are you willingly participative, observant and aware of what is going on around you, good at suggesting ideas, moving forward – or are you sometimes blind-sided and feel that you often arrive late to the issues?

TECHNIQUES FOR CULTIVATING PROACTIVITY

✓ Empower yourself to move forward.

✓ Don't wait to be told what to do, take the initiative – create, don't wait!

✓ Forward-focus on the big picture, and less on the immediate problems.

✓ Be confident, don't doubt yourself – take the first step and begin.

✓ Stay focused on solutions, not on the problem.

✓ Plan ahead; think about what needs to be done long-term and what needs to be done short-term, and in that context, what needs to be done next.

✓ Prevent small issues turning into big problems. When challenges approach, take control and confront them head on before they grow into overwhelming problems.

✓ Get good at scanning the business and work landscape and being able to predict potential happenings. Anticipate what could happen next, and try to stay one step ahead. Don't always expect the past to be an accurate predictor of the future.

Be Energizing

Being a future shaper requires high energy – from you and your team – to sustain the necessary motivation and a drive to achieve your goals. Consider how you could cultivate the capacity to energize yourself first, and then think about how to energize others. It starts with you and whether you feel connected to a higher vision and purpose. How passionate and motivated are you about your preferable outcome and what you want to achieve? If you feel energized by what you do, then you will be able to inspire and energize other people to follow you and support you in achieving the preferable outcomes. If you are passionate about your goals, a natural process of emotional contagion will do a lot of the work for you in relation to how you affect and energize other people.

If you feel energized by what you do, then you will be able to inspire and energize other people.

Emotional contagion is the phenomenon of having one person's emotions and related behaviours directly trigger similar emotions and behaviours in other people. Followers consciously or unconsciously copy the mood and behaviours of the leader. They follow the leader. Your positive (or negative) energy and emotion will automatically spread virally to your team and stakeholders through what you say and how you behave.

As a simple example of emotional contagion: if the boss wakes up in a bad mood, unless the boss can regulate their emotions, everyone has a bad mood that day! Conversely if the boss is consistently highly motivated, and has high energy, high inspiration, then team productivity can be very positively virally affected. Your awareness of leadership emotional contagion is important – it means you need to be more responsible about how you regulate and manage your own emotions in the workplace, at meetings, on conference calls; it also means you have more power than you realize to positively affect the mood and attitude of your team and others.

Not a lot of leadership textbooks talk about the importance of the happy leader but if you are not happy in your role, how can you inspire and energize others? Being joyful and feeling fulfilled at work is an optimal zone for great work. In a world of obstacles and challenges, it is too easy to become negative, miserable and unproductive. It takes more effort and conscious work to reframe obstacles and challenges as growth opportunities, and to meet them as a happy, creative and productive problem-solver – and to really mean it!

Even when you have a higher mission, it is not always easy to maintain high energy. Build a good support system around you – friends, family and professional people who can nurture you and support you to maintain a healthy perspective. Invest in self-care to sustain a healthy body, healthy mind and healthy spirit as a future shaper. Sustain a positive outlook and perform your role in a way that is meaningful to you and makes you happy.

The energizing trait is about having purpose and this is critical to the 'preferable' component of the future shaper framework. Uncertainty and adversity are more easily put into perspective if the future shaper has the energy to withstand them, and can energize their people to stay focused on the bigger picture. This is your choice – do you choose to be high energy and energizing;

TABLE 9.1 Which leader are you?

Energizing	Not energizing
✓ Good listening skills	✗ Self-involved
✓ Strong communication skills	✗ No gratitude
✓ Generous with time and ideas	✗ Lack of passion
✓ Commitment to development of team	✗ Lack of purpose
	✗ Cannot be trusted
✓ Genuine passion and excitement about the work	✗ Poor listening skills
	✗ Poor communication skills
	✗ Negative attitude/pessimism
✓ Appreciation for the team members' hard work	✗ No interest in developing people
✓ Positivity/an optimism and belief in future better states	✗ No compelling vision of the future
✓ Clear vision of the future and what could be achieved, eg 'I have a dream'	

or do you choose to be swamped and overloaded by the external events of the day and week? Are you driven by an intrinsic mission that fuels you and renews you? Or are you run ragged by external events in control of you?

As a future shaper, you need to inspire, enthuse and motivate those around you so that they bring their A-game and want to stay working for you:

- Do you feel connected to your leadership purpose?
- Do you find your work meaningful and fulfilling?
- Do you have an optimistic, glass-half-full attitude?

Be Resourceful

Resourcefulness is about the creative ability to overcome problems and making do with what is available to develop a solution. Resourcefulness and innovation go hand in hand. It is the ability to find quick and clever ways to overcome difficulties, solve problems or find creative new ideas and solutions. It requires creative, agile thinking. As humans, we have a basic instinct to survive and as such, we all have a level of resourcefulness when it comes to survival and thriving, so you definitely have it. Just be more alert to using it! Sometimes people only become really resourceful when under extreme pressure – but I want to surface resourcefulness as a must-have leadership trait for your future shaper toolkit day to day rather than waiting for an extreme situation. Being resourceful is an attitude as well as an action – it is about being open-minded, having a problem-solving mental-ity, rejecting limits and not taking every 'no' as a first answer.

Resourcefulness is about problem-solving, creativity and adaptability:

- Problem-solving – your ability to devise quick and clever solutions.
- Creativity – keeping an open mind about a range of possibilities.
- Adaptability – ability to adapt to deliver, even when the goalposts change.

Aggressive competition for available budget and people means we all have to learn to make do with what we have. Being resourceful is partly about doing more with less, and also about squeezing more potential and capability from you and your people to find new creative ways to solve problems and achieve your goals. You can do more with less because you and your colleagues are probably more capable than you can ever believe. Resourcefulness is not just a means of coping with deprivation; it can be a virtue that opens the door to greater accomplishment. Be open-minded and redefine the possible.

Resourcefulness is most important when it comes to the 'prove' part of the future shaper framework. It is about how you and your team are going to execute your plans, and do what it takes to get things done. Role modelling your resourcefulness

FIGURE 9.2 Examples of resourcefulness

Is there another way?

What would someone else do?

Ask

Who else could help me?

Is there one more thing I could try?

and praising others for being resourceful can become part of your culture and embedded in your ways of working:

- Are you open-minded about the possibilities?
- Can you see the potential in every situation?
- Are you able to think outside the box, think laterally and think creatively?
- Are you good at finding ways to do what it takes to achieve your goals?

TECHNIQUES FOR CULTIVATING RESOURCEFULNESS

✓ Get good at evaluating the situation and what you have available to tackle the issues. Check whether you are faced with the problem or a symptom of a bigger problem. Is solving the symptom merely 'fire-fighting' and do you need to focus resources on solving the bigger problem too?

✓ Think creatively – is there another way? Adapt your ideas and prior experience to bring fresh thinking to the table.

✓ When someone puts a limit on you, push back – don't take the first 'no' as the final answer.

✓ Negotiate better – how can you get what you want, and achieve a win for the other person too?

✓ Who else can help – think about who has access to the resources you need. For example, can you borrow someone temporarily from another team?

✓ Be prepared to bend the rules – sometimes in pursuit of the right outcome, it is better to ask for forgiveness later, than ask for permission in advance, knowing you will be told 'No'.

✓ Dare to ask for what you want and need – if you don't ask, you don't get.

✓ Keep your options open – play a few hands at the same time, so you have a few options in play to help solve the problem or overcome the obstacle.

✓ Embrace different possibilities, opportunities, people, views, suggestions and experiences.

Think about how to cultivate these F.U.T.U.R.E. S.H.A.P.E.R. traits in yourself and within your team. As a leader, you can't exist in isolation from your team, and your team is the best compensating mechanism for any weaknesses or gaps in your own competency. So, as you read through each future shaper trait, think about whether you possess it and whether as a group your team possesses it, and at what level – high, medium or low (see Table 9.2). Consider how you and your team can best complement each other in the pursuit of the total.

F.U.T.U.R.E. S.H.A.P.E.R. traits are about improving your leadership character, and character is what matters in leadership. Character is about who you are, and not just about the results you achieve. With this in mind, as a final wrap on important

TABLE 9.2   F.U.T.U.R.E. S.H.A.P.E.R. traits – self assessment

	High	Medium	Low
Fearless			
Unifying			
Tenacious			
Unconventional			
Resilient			
Empathetic			
Super-adaptable			
Hard-working			
Authentic			
Proactive			
Energizing			
Resourceful			

future shaper leadership traits, of course it is critical for the future shaper to be honest and have integrity. Take that as a given. Unfortunately, following a series of corporate scandals, the word 'integrity' on a list of leadership traits has completely lost its cachet, because these corrupt companies all cited integrity on their lists of company values! There has been so much lack of integrity by some people in charge, that the word 'integrity' has lost its integrity. I am going to assume you know it is important to be honest, not to break the law, to role model good morals and values, and to hold yourself accountable to a set of high standards of behaviour expected by your teams and by society.

The five fundamentals are about what you do, and the F.U.T.U.R.E. S.H.A.P.E.R. traits are about your character and the way you use those fundamentals. Consider the suggested techniques and decide what strategies you need to deploy to better cultivate these traits in yourself and your team.

PART FIVE

Shape a better future for everyone

CHAPTER TEN

Create a positive ripple effect on the world around you

Collaborate with other future shapers – and change the world

I hope by now you feel inspired and equipped to be a future shaper leader, but don't feel that you have to push everything forward on your own. I know from experience that, even with a great team, leaders sometimes feel too isolated, or feel unsupported at peer level in their roles. Be assured that you are not alone in wanting to shape a better future, driven by more meaningfulness and more purposeful future outcomes. There are other people who also want to make a difference. Seek out the support and companionship of like-minded fellow members of your future shaper tribe and collaborate on your shared ideas. Together you can ideate, shape and influence positive business change. Rather than feel isolated or as if you're on a solo crusade, reach out to find your fellow future shapers and together make an even bigger impact.

You might find such people in your company or in your current circle of contacts. Key industry conferences and events are great places to go in search of your tribe. Whatever your area of interest, there is likely to be an annual conference on the topic where keynote speakers will help enhance your understanding – and where you can meet like-minded peers and interested parties. You could become a member of a peer-to-peer learning community in your area or online. If your ideas are so niche or so avant garde that no one is addressing them, then consider setting up your own conference or meet-up group and invite your preferred guests to attend.

FIND YOUR TRIBE

Collaborate with other like-minded future shapers. If you can find and build your tribe, this will build your leverage for achieving shared preferables. Think about the people you consider to be expert and who you trust and admire. Perhaps you can share your ideas and spark off each other to get your ideas off the ground. Future shaper leadership does not need to be a lonely sport – join forces with like-minded leaders, as long as you are co-creating for optimization and not sacrificing ideas for the sake of consensus building. In the same way that many great businesses required more than one founder to get them off the ground, your future shaping efforts may be enhanced by having a partner or partners right from the beginning:

✓ Share each other's network and platforms.

✓ Help each other to progress ideas and resources.

✓ Sense-check your ideas with other future shapers.

✓ Tap into the wisdom and energy of the collective.

✓ Engage constructively with what others are also trying to achieve.

Consider the enormous value that could be unlocked by tribes of future shaper leaders coming together to collaborate on shared outcomes. Imagine if the leaders of every organization empowered themselves to set out a higher big-picture vision of future preferable outcomes and aligned their teams and energy behind achieving these outcomes – and also helped and supported each other to achieve a better future for everyone. Against a backdrop of all the problems that need to be tackled in the world, imagine if every business leader in every organization chose to step up and make a positive purposeful leadership difference during their window of power. Major world change would be achievable. The crisis of climate change could be a collaborative future shaping focus. The crisis of inequality could be a collaborative future shaping focus. Business leaders could step up and help fill some of the gaps left by politicians on improving the state of our world.

Collectively all those positive differences would create a momentum shift and a tipping point into a new, more positive version of our world. How great it would be if this book was the catalyst for a future shaping movement across the world. A time when a global community of leaders realize they are not at the mercy of events happening to them – and that they have more power than they realize to take charge and set out ambitious courses of action that truly shape the future. We have the imagination, we have the technology, this book provides a guiding framework – all we need now is the will to do it.

How great it would be if this book was the catalyst for a future shaping movement across the world.

The timing is ripe for this kind of business leadership momentum shift. There is already significant pressure on business leaders to evolve their role and be a force for good for society. A societal appetite exists to see business leaders play a more value-adding role in improving the way the world works and lives. It is no longer good enough for business leaders to focus on just making a profit. They must also earn and sustain public trust to earn their social licence to operate. Business leaders need to pay attention not only to competing on value but to also contributing value to the society. The more highly regulated the industry, the more important this becomes as the price of entry or the price of staying in business.

Consider the tremendous possibilities and positive future for our world if all global CEOs and top business leaders collaborated during their window of power to be a positive future shaping force for good for business and society – in parallel with their day job of leading their organization. Big-picture, big-world topics could be addressed that would improve the planet we all live on. It would also transform the global brand and reputation of big business. If future shaping became a global CEO and business leadership movement, then its combined collective membership could be a huge force for good in our world – shaping futures for our generation and future generations.

Today there is more open distrust of big business and big government than ever before. Corruption and tax avoidance scandals have damaged previously much-loved brands and left customers disillusioned with global business. More recently we see that the tech entrepreneurs who were lauded for their clever innovations and speed to market are now also facing a backlash on trust and data privacy issues, and more serious allegations of how social media platforms are being used to manipulate political elections. These corporate scandals are less and less tolerated by a more sophisticated and more educated customer population. Social media fuels brand fires, and your organization might just face total wipeout if you do not have a sufficient reservoir of trust with your customers and stakeholders. A list of nice-to-have corporate values and corporate social responsibility as pretty 'window dressing' is not acceptable to employees and customers any more. While there is tremendous pressure from customers to improve the speed, convenience and price of products and services, there is also

TABLE 10.1   The potential transformation of the business leader role to future shaper leader

From profit-focus: 'make a profit and do no harm to the world'	To beyond-profit focus: 'make a profit and add value to the world'
CEOs and business leaders are paid to run their organization, hit quarterly targets, drive shareholder value and deliver high return on investment.	CEOs and business leaders are expected to do more than just make a profit. They are expected to develop ambitious visions of the future and contribute to the greater good of society.
It is not the job of the business leader to solve the problems of the world. That is the role of government, the United Nations and other global non-profit organizations.	It is the role of the business leader to step up and solve global leadership problems, especially when the politicians narrow the definition of their roles to become overly concerned with national problems.
Making a difference is only an extra-curricular 'nice-to-have' activity for brand and reputation, to which leaders arbitrarily opt in or out of investing time, energy and resources.	Making a difference is synonymous with good business leadership, and becomes the price of market entry for socially-minded consumers of today.

pressure to do good business, while avoiding harm to the planet and exploitation of workers. We all want better, faster, safer, cheaper products and services, but there is also an appetite for a transformational change; for the CEOs and business leaders to take up their position as member leaders of the world, and to use their window of power for the greater good, beyond a narrow definition of just making a profit.

POTENTIAL G7-STYLE FUTURE SHAPER COLLABORATIONS

CEOs and top business leaders have mutual concerns on a range of topic areas that offer a rich source of future shaping G7-style collaborations: for example, topic areas such as growth, risk, regulatory management, technology, innovation, people and resources.

Future shaper CEOs could choose to convene G7-style to collaborate on how to future shape and address and solve big topics. For example, connected by a common concern for the deterioration of natural resources available to us all, their collective preferable outcome could be 'to improve planetary health' and they could agree on subset target outcomes in the categories of:

- climate change;
- food safety;
- security (national, international, digital, non-digital);
- water supply;
- clean air;
- energy.

Their platform of power and influence, with a further multiplier of collaboration, could truly shape the future of our world for the better, and fast. These could be big breakthrough leadership legacy ideas that last beyond their tenure and will have lasting sustainable long-term value to benefit everybody.

This is not just a utopian vision of the future – it could actually happen, if we choose to make it happen. If *you* choose to make it happen. That is the essence of future shaping leadership – you decide the kind of future you want to shape, and you go for it until you succeed. There is nothing stopping any business leader from instigating what I describe above, other than purpose and platform, and the skills and desire to persuade, persist and prove.

The reason why it is not already happening is tragically simple: business executives are not yet incentivized to do anything other than fulfil a narrow definition of their leadership role, ie maximize shareholder value by delivering agreed business targets. Unfortunately there is currently a lack of understanding about the link between shareholder value and societal value, and the concept of social licence to operate is not yet fully recognized. However, this is changing; stakeholder and shareholder models need not be in conflict and a new generation will eventually look back in disbelief that this link was ever questioned. Already there are some businesses that are set up with the widest stakeholder understanding in mind – referred to as social impact businesses. There are also green shoots of understanding within the corporate world that treating all stakeholders well is in shareholders' interest, and we see some examples of companies closely monitoring their societal impact, and reporting transparently on this impact.

The future shaper knows that responsible business is good for business; building competitive advantage, reputation and legitimacy. Responsible business practices, in addition to avoiding costs, can help to build a positive corporate culture and image. This in turn can influence the retention of employees; help increase productivity as well as boost corporate and product brand appeal and thus increase market strength and position. Responsible business conduct means that businesses should make a positive contribution to economic, environmental and social progress with a view to achieving sustainable development, and that businesses have a responsibility to avoid and address the adverse impacts of their operations. While the concept of corporate social responsibility is often associated with philanthropic corporate conduct external to business operations, responsible business conduct goes beyond this to emphasize integration of responsible practices within internal operations and throughout business relationships and supply chains (Nieuwenkamp, 2016).

As a future shaper leader, ask yourself if there is something you can do to transform the core issues in your team, your organization, your industry, your world. If talking about changing the world feels too intimidating or grandiose to you, then focus on what you want to do to change your world – the domain and ecosystem within which your day, month, year happens. Take up your position as a leader in your world, be prepared to stand up and stand out as a future shaper leader in your role, your team and your organization.

Empower yourself, empower others to shape a better future

The central message of this book is 'empowerment'. If you take nothing else away from this book, just take this simple message: don't wait for someone else to tell you what to do. Create, don't wait. Create your own future. Realize that you have more power than you think to shape the future you desire, and to shape the world we live in. If you experience problems with the current state of affairs, don't waste energy on blame or expect others to fix any mess. Decide what you are going to do about it. When you feel empowered, you feel more in control and it is so much easier for you to empower other people. From a place of feeling secure with your purpose, you will be more expansive about encouraging other people to find their meaningfulness in work. You will help others to solve small and big problems in their own way, and work to the best of their collective ability.

Don't wait for someone else to tell you what to do.

Success will come from understanding and appreciating that you, as leader, are not expected to know everything and do all the telling. The world is just too complex for you to have all the answers and leaders can no longer lead as if the knowledge and power is centralized in them. Instead, your role will be to assemble the best teams, and harness the energy and creativity and strengths of your teams to understand and solve problems. Empower yourself to think big and be ambitious, and empower other people to creatively ideate with you to solve and deliver on ambitions. Trust and empower and support your team to fulfil their individual and collective potential. Empowerment is a means to include the team in decision making, to give them a participatory role that capitalizes on their own expertise and judgement, which in turn increases their sense of both individual worth and commitment to the preferable outcome.

To relinquish traditional control, but still hold yourself and others accountable requires you, the leader, to:

- Share your vision.
- Trust yourself.
- Trust your team members.
- Give opportunities and autonomy.
- Check for understanding of the task.
- Foster skills, passions and creativity.
- Share information, share your knowledge.
- Expect mistakes along the way and reframe as learning.
- Stop micro-managing, but do regularly check in and provide support.
- Empower, but don't abdicate responsibility; continue to hold people accountable.

It's hard to believe but some leaders still see information as power – and something they withhold from their people and teams, so that only they have the bigger picture and full context. Of course, some information will be sensitive and not for sharing, but truly great leaders do not manipulate people by withholding information just for the sake of a power trip – or worse, to prevent other people from shining. Sharing information builds trust and can help the people on your teams to make better decisions.

Empowering people is mainly a trust exercise – one that yields positive results. High-trust people are generally very secure about their own boundaries, and willing to assume – in the first instance – that others are equally as trustworthy. Of course, the wisdom on trust includes not being naïve about the fact that some people are not trustworthy and sometimes the most charming of people are the least trustworthy of all! Trusting others doesn't mean you abdicate your leadership responsibility. You must always hold people accountable to a high set of standards. Give autonomy to those who have shown they can handle it. Check in, expect updates and keep communication flowing. When we encourage people to take risks, we need to stay loyal when those risks don't pan out. Create a learning environment whereby teams regularly reflect on progress, failures and lessons learned on what to do differently (or not) the next time.

Succeed in your leadership career and make an impact

What matters to most people is to create a future that's filled with success, achievement and happiness. However, when it comes down to doing the work, many either procrastinate or don't give it their all or simply lose interest when the going gets tough. Unfortunately we all have a tendency to set goals and forget them rather than setting goals and working tirelessly towards their fruition. The problem is that anything in life that's worthwhile takes a lot of work. Becoming a future shaper won't be easy by any means. If you want to be a future shaper leader and shape a bigger and brighter future, you have to be willing to put in the energy and effort. You will need to be good at persuading people to follow you, and you will need to be persistent and resilient in the face of any challenges. You need to build a winning team and get results. You also need to put yourself out there and power up your network so that you build up your position of influence. You will also need to cultivate the kind of leadership traits that have become relevant for now, with special emphasis on fearlessness and resilience. The effort will be worth it because you will be working on your dreams to shape a better future and add real leadership value to the world.

When I think about the world we live in, I am filled with optimism. It may be very reductionist but what helps me is to realize that the world is just made up of people and the decisions they take. Some people have more power than others – and they are the 'leaders' of all the other people. So, it follows that if our leaders strive to do a better job and evolve their leadership skills and approach – then we can all take better control of the problems facing our world. Whenever the commentators talk about economic crisis and world problems, don't fall into the trap of seeing these as external events happening to us. See them as symptoms of a leadership problem, a failure of good-quality leadership, poor decision making and a lack of unified problem solving. See yourself as someone who can do something to lead others into a better future.

Let's take a look at the leaders who are admired and considered successful right now. It makes for a fun conversation – often hotly debated – to decide on who should make the list of the top 10 CEOs who shape our world today, or indeed the historic top 10 leaders who had a significant impact. Table 10.2 is not a definitive top 10 – these are just examples to get you thinking about the kinds of future shapers past and present who have made their mark.

It would be interesting and humbling for the business community, and some of the richest people on the planet, to realize that many in the column on the left will never actually make it into the column on the right. Notice that very few CEOs' names or legacies really stand the test of time. Many business leaders are dominating our attention today, but are they making a really lasting future shaping legacy? Perhaps there is more to world future shaping than building a big business and dominating their markets. Don't confuse market dominance with true future shaping.

TABLE 10.2 Admired leaders – past and present

Examples of CEOs and leaders who influence and shape the world we live in today	Examples of historic leaders who shaped the future of our world
• Tim Cook, Apple • Jeff Bezos, Amazon • Elon Musk, SpaceX • Oprah Winfrey, Harpo Studios • Larry Page and Sergey Brin, Google founders • Mark Zuckerberg, Facebook • Jack Ma, Alibaba founder • Muhammad Yunus, Grameen Bank • Paul Polman, ex-Unilever • Jack Dorsey, Twitter	• Martin Luther King Jr • Nelson Mandela • Albert Einstein • Mahatma Gandhi • Charles Darwin • Christopher Columbus • Marie Curie • Henry Ford • Thomas Edison • Emmeline Pankhurst

Perhaps you will be on this list one day. Our world needs our business leaders to try harder, to take more responsibility, to deliver better outcomes faster. I encourage the emergence of a new breed of leader – future shapers – who will take their leadership role very seriously, who will create positive change out of chaos, who will lead by example, and who will motivate their teams and others to deliver on missions that will strengthen their organizations and help boost the economy. With each leader more finely attuned and focused on delivering meaningful lasting leadership legacies, positive change will come.

The way I see it is that one person can change the world, and that type of person is a true leader.

Perhaps you think you are not important enough to matter, that one person cannot change the world. Or that you are too junior to make an impact in your massively matrixed organization. Perhaps you feel that you have the ideas but no platform, no voice to be heard and no one listening anyway. The way I see it is that one person can change the world, and that type of person is a true leader. The way I see it is that most people underestimate what they are capable of. Whatever your role, whatever your organization – if you step up as a future shaper leader, you can make a lasting impact. Leadership has become more democratized, less hierarchical. Command and control structures of the past have given way to flatter organization and flatter power-sharing in the organizations. Leadership can come from anywhere – from the digital-native graduate new-joiner, to the newly promoted leader in a large corporate, to the entrepreneurial college drop-out. It comes from within the person who dares to dream of creating a better future and who dares to decide to make a difference.

You, dear reader, can be the one to make a difference. I encourage you to be open to and curious about what is being suggested in this book – and to apply what you learn to step up and become a future shaper leader. Become someone who is unafraid to lead, unafraid to imagine what is possible, unafraid to rally cry to others and secure their support. Become a leader who has purpose, who can inspire others, who is willing to persist when the path appears to be blocked – always asking, is there another way? Become someone who can build great teams, achieve great results and is savvy about how to secure the kind of platform and power base required, in order to be heard.

The world needs you to lead for good, and create a better future for you and for all of us, now more than ever before. I wish you well on your future shaping mission.

References

Chapter 1

Business & Sustainable Development Commission (2017) Better Business, Better World [online] http://report.businesscommission.org/report (archived at https://perma.cc/5Q73-XXXR) [accessed 12 November 2019]

Schwab, K (2016) The Fourth Industrial Revolution, Portfolio Penguin

Solomon, M (2016) You've got millennial employees all wrong; here are the four things you need to know now, Forbes, 26 January [online] www.forbes.com/sites/micahsolomon/2016/01/26/everything-youve-heard-about-millennial-employees-is-baloney-heres-the-truth-and-how-to-use-it/#23514b564904 (archived at https://perma.cc/3TJS-QQ37) [accessed 12 November 2019]

Chapter 2

Gladwell, M (2008) Outliers: The story of success, Allen Lane

Chapter 4

Obama, M (2015) Let girls learn, The Atlantic, 2 November [online] www.theatlantic.com/international/archive/2015/11/girls-education-michelle-obama/413554/ (archived at https://perma.cc/FF2H-CEPX) [accessed 12 November 2019]

Chapter 5

Deutschendorf, H (2015) 7 Habits of highly persistent people, Fast Company, 1 April [online] www.fastcompany.com/3044531/7-habits-of-highly-persistent-people (archived at https://perma.cc/6TMJ-KSJX) [accessed 12 November 2019]

Chapter 6

Daugherty, P, Carrel-Billiard, M and Biltz, M (2019) Empower the human+ worker, accenture, 7 February [online] www.accenture.com/us-en/insights/technology/future-of-work (archived at https://perma.cc/B3VG-3U3P) [accessed 12 November 2019]

Chapter 7

Aron, J (2018) Stephen Hawking: Tributes pour in as physicist dies aged 76, *New Scientist*, 14 March [online] www.newscientist.com/article/2163649-stephen-hawking-tributes-pour-in-as-physicist-dies-aged-76 (archived at https://perma.cc/QNR9-S7DG) [accessed 12 November 2019]

Hawking, S (2018) *Brief Answers to the Big Questions*, John Murray

Jarrett, M (2017) The 4 types of organizational politics, *Harvard Business Review*, 24 April [online] https://hbr.org/2017/04/the-4-types-of-organizational-politics (archived at https://perma.cc/5LVP-FEA5) [accessed 12 November 2019]

Sherman, R O (2013) Why reputation is your most important leadership asset, *Emerging RN Leader*, 14 January [online] www.emergingrnleader.com/why-reputation-is-your-most-important-leadership-asset/ (archived at https://perma.cc/898H-CRKV) [accessed 12 November 2019]

Wiseman, R (2019) *Shoot for the Moon*, Quercus

Chapter 10

Nieuwenkamp, R (2016) Landmark human rights cases show value of OECD grievance mechanism for responsible business, Friends of the OECD Guidelines for Multinational Enterprises, 25 August [online] https://friendsoftheoecdguidelines.wordpress.com/tag/corporate-social-responsibility (archived at https://perma.cc/ZNU7-WV6A) [accessed 12 November 2019]

Index